Advance  Spiritual Tra... Emotional Intelligence and Freedom

In a world in which interpersonal relationships have become increasingly depersonalized due to social media, the ability to identify and manage one's own emotions (as well as the emotions of others) is becoming a lost skill. This skill, known as emotional intelligence, is an essential tool for disciples of Jesus, who have been tasked by God to appeal to the hearts and souls of others, in an effort to win them over and share the good news of salvation. Like other aptitudes, EQ falls on a normal curve: some people have a great deal of natural EQ, and others have less. Fortunately, EQ can be understood, learned, and developed. In her book, Cresenda Jones guides the reader to a better understanding of the theory and science of EQ, while also providing very practical, Bible-based exercises to improve EQ and progress toward greater spiritual, social, and emotional maturity. A must-have book for anyone who deals with people, which is pretty much everyone!

—Michael S. Shapiro, PhD, author of *Rejoice Always*

Cresenda Jones, in her book *Spiritual Transformation: Emotional Intelligence and Freedom,* brings to the reader a useful, readable approach to shaping our emotions into what God intends for them to be. While our IQ never changes much, our EQ, so important in almost every area of life, can change significantly. Ms. Jones provides us with a well-researched book filled with Scripture, science, testimonials, and practicals for achieving an emotionally healthy life that will be a joy to ourselves and those around us.

—Al Baird, Elder, Phoenix Church of Christ

It's always refreshing to come across resources and material aimed at helping you to be your best. I especially appreciate all the time and research that went into this very helpful and inspiring resource. As someone who has been battling depression for several years, I connected with the information in Chapter 4, "Master Your Mind." Understanding how my brain works and processes my thoughts and emotions, and eventually my actions, has encouraged me to pursue "mastering my mind!" The reflection questions are very helpful with this. Cresenda Jones has put together a valuable resource that I believe will help many of God's children in their pursuit to love him with all their heart, soul, mind, and strength.

—James R. Warren Jr., Evangelist, NYC Church of Christ Harlem Region

One of the constant criticisms leveled against Christian forays into the world of psychology or emotional intelligence is that they are worldly and not rooted in Scripture. Cresenda Jones has avoided that problem in this book. *Spiritual Transformation: Emotional Intelligence and Freedom* combines the best theories and practices that are available regarding emotional intelligence, but roots everything in Scripture from beginning to end. If you are interested in this area of growth, you will not be disappointed.

—Michael Burns, Biblical Teacher, Two Cities Church (Minneapolis)

I enjoyed reading Cresenda Jones' new book, *Spiritual Maturity: Emotional Intelligence and Freedom* very much! Chapter 4 is especially fascinating about the brain's plasticity and our ability to rewire our emotions from past events. This workbook is full of scriptures and practical strategies to help us intentionally focus on growing spiritually. I plan on using this workbook in several ways: first as a personal tool to help myself grow in my own emotional intelligence and also in working with women in the church and clients in private practice who want to learn more about recognizing, understanding, and managing their emotions.

—Cathy Marutzky, M.Ed., LPCC, NCC

Who doesn't want increased spiritual maturity and emotional intelligence? Though we desire such maturity and intelligence, it can often elude us. Cresenda Jones, in her information-rich workbook on spiritual transformation, makes this elusive maturity more accessible, as she not only shares her own life journey of transformation but also her knowledge gained through years of vigorous study. Personal testimonies and reflection questions allow the reader to both relate to the discussion and apply it to their own lives. This workbook gives each reader an opportunity to gain much-needed courage and helpful tools for growth, resulting in increased emotional and spiritual transformation.

—Jeanie Shaw, Women's Minister, Author

In the past few years, emotional awareness has increased while biblical knowledge has decreased. This book has both, and is powerful, cogent, and useful for our current cultural climate. With solid biblical principles, it has a plethora of resources and a mixture of grace and truth that is truly encouraging. It is a workbook that works—on many different levels. As a minister, I found myself inspired to focus more on my EQ to better serve others in their emotional maturity.

—Leke Lewu, Evangelist, One Miami Church

Continued spiritual growth and transformation into the likeness of Christ is like oxygen to the soul. When we "get stuck" and hit road blocks, the growth and transformation can stall, which can leave us doubting and discouraged. *Spiritual Transformation* is a great resource and will shed light on and bring hope and answers to those searching to break free. The information, reflection questions, and supporting material will guide you to a rich understanding of your emotions and how to best show up in life. Many times in our Christian walk, we need tools to help us get to that next level—to get "unstuck." This is your manual to do just that!

—Dave Mitchell, Certified High-Performance Coach

Cresenda Jones is a dynamic author and speaker who has dedicated her life to helping others understand and connect with their true self-worth in the eyes of God. This takes understanding and deconstructing the layers built by lifelong experiences and emotions. Her new book, *Spiritual Transformation: Emotional Intelligence and Freedom,* is a power-packed workbook to step-by-step develop your emotional intelligence quotient and learn to recognize, understand, and manage your emotions. This allows one the freedom to accept all emotions as part of our God-given nature, and to choose to mature in the godly direction of managing our emotions to love ourselves and build up one another in love. This takes work! Awareness is just the first step! Cresenda Jones will walk you through the challenging process of facing your emotions and understanding them, and practicing mindful change. Her goal is genuine connection—to yourself, to God, and to your world. This is a crucial read for the Christian and every person who longs for true spiritual growth.

—Cynthia A. Darby, M.Ed., Ed.S., LCMHC, Licensed Clinical Mental Health Counselor

God built us to be healthy and free on the inside. He modeled it, illustrated it, and equipped us for it. In order to love God deeply and to be serious about loving others just as Jesus loves us, we cannot neglect growing in EQ. This book will inform you and set you on the path of growing in EQ to become emotionally healthy and help others along the way. This will not leave any relationship unaffected.

—Keith Winship, Minister, Clemson Foothills Church

Cresenda Jones' newest book, *Spiritual Transformation: Emotional Intelligence and Freedom,* is thoughtful, vulnerable, and skillfully written. Cresenda practically applies biblical truths to understanding our emotions and provides insight into how to "be transformed by the renewing of [our] minds" and hearts. Readers will be guided into steps to grow in emotional intelligence as well as understanding that growth in EQ is essential to spiritual maturity in relationships with God, others, and self. I am thankful for the professional and spiritual relationship that Cresenda and I now enjoy and feel privileged to have a first look at *Spiritual Transformation.* I highly recommend this book for all who want to grow in their ability to relate to God, themselves, and others on an emotionally mature level.

—Beverly Ozanne, MAMFC, LPC, LCDC, Licensed Professional Counselor/Pastoral Counselor

As always, Cresenda Jones offers us a masterful and practical roadmap to spiritual maturity. *Spiritual Transformation: Emotional Intelligence and Freedom* deserves a place on every Christian's bookshelf.

—Rick Maule, Minister, Elder, and Award-winning Author

We need HELP! We need LOVE! We need a SPIRITUAL TRANSFORMATION! Knowing why we need them lies within this book. Cresenda Jones' vulnerability and expertise allows you to understand why we have emotions, how to understand our emotions, and how to develop the necessary skills to reach a healthy level of emotional intelligence. We aren't doomed to depression, negative thoughts, or feelings of insignificance. God has plans for you and me. We can overcome. Cresenda's book is just the beginning. We were made for such a time as this!

—Dontaye Carter, Carter Media Group Founder

This book is for everyone! How one deals with their emotional intelligence will determine their wholistic well-being. There is a shift in the scientific world that recognizes a person's emotional intelligence (EQ) as far more important than their IQ. Cresenda Jones' book has very helpful tools that will help Christians learn how to navigate their emotions by recognizing them, understanding them, and learning how to manage them using the Scriptures. It not only gives you facts about emotions; it will allow you to draw closer to God and let you know that God, the Author of emotions, understands what you are going through. He is always with you and will guide you through these emotional times. For a quick understanding of what EQ is, see the list "this book is for you" in the introduction.

—Bertha Chukwueke, Women's Ministry Leader, Greater Baltimore Church of Christ

This is just what we need, and timely! We will be using this scripture-filled book along with the *Emotional Intelligence 2.0* Appraisal as our outside resource during the Disciples In Motion session beginning this weekend. Thank you, Cresenda!

—Alan and Sherry Rouse, Elder and wife, Atlanta Church of Christ in Gwinnett, Georgia

Cresenda Jones is a powerhouse leader in the worlds of emotional intelligence and biblical personal development. From an authentic personal testimony to a powerful example of overcoming obstacle after obstacle, Cresenda will have you on the edge of your seat awaiting your next dose of pure, unadulterated Holy Spirit–led inspiration to overcome.

—Michelle Curtis, Women's Ministry, Greater Houston Church

When I saw that Cresenda Jones' book was about emotional intelligence (EQ), my initial reaction was "Ughh." That is likely because my normally quiet Dad once told me, "Men don't cry. Men don't show emotion..." However, I was impressed with her writing and appreciated her candor. I love the application of Scripture to the topic at hand and her use of Scripture to point out emotions of people in the Bible along with those of Jesus Christ and God. I also loved the comparison of Scripture references from different Bible translations. The questions for deeper insight and discussion are great. I was personally convicted when Cresenda asked, in more than one chapter, "How many questions do you ask before expressing an opinion?" I have decided to be more intent in that area. Lastly, I appreciated learning about the four parts of EQ, and the need for social awareness especially stood out for me.

—Eddie Francis, Elder & Evangelist, Orlando Church of Christ

In her most recent book, *Spiritual Transformation: Intelligence and Freedom*, Cresenda Jones continues to demonstrate her passion for God's people. Ms. Jones has devoted much of her adult life championing emotional health. She has tackled the subject of mental health in the faith community with missionary zeal. As a result, she has carefully crafted this text with tons of practical resources and biblical grounding for all who seek spiritual transformation. This is a must-read.

—Will Archer, Evangelist, Potomac Valley Church

This is a powerful book! Cresenda Jones thoroughly and practically examines many of the processes of spiritual transformation through the lenses of Scripture, Emotional Intelligence (EQ), Neuro-Linguistic Programming (NLP) and Time Line Therapy®. Cresenda describes, compares and integrates these approaches and explains exactly how they can lead to spiritual transformation. This book is saturated in Scripture, and also features several personal case studies written by Christians who are applying and benefiting from many of the principles included in this book. Cover-to-cover, this book is full of helpful ideas, questions, teaching, and practices for individuals as well as practitioners, coaches, therapists, counselors, ministers and anyone else who is responsible for the care of souls and for helping people to grow so as to become more and more like Jesus.

—Joey Harris, Co-Director, Athens Institute of Ministry (AIM)

Spiritual Transformation

Transformation

Emotional Intelligence and Freedom

Cresenda Jones

ISBN: 978-1-948450-90-4. Printed in the United States.

All Scripture quotations, unless indicated, are taken from the Holy Bible, New International Version®, NIV® Copyright ©1973, 1978, 1984, 2011 by Biblica, Inc.® Used by permission. All rights reserved worldwide.

Since there is a wealth of scriptures in this workbook, a full list of the Scripture references and passages for each chapter is posted on my website (www.cresendajones.com).

Interior design and layout by Toney C. Mulhollan and cover design by Roy Appelsamy of Toronto, Canada.

About the author: Cresenda Jones, a counselor and life coach, has been a disciple since 1986, in North Carolina, Georgia, Pennsylvania, New Jersey, and Florida churches of Christ. Generational trauma and dysfunction led her to intently seek both spiritual maturity and emotional health. Along the journey, her MA in professional counseling, MBA, and M.Ed have provided clearer roadmaps and growth. She considers it a privilege to witness growth and miraculous transformations when she facilitates the Time Line Therapy® breakthrough process, discussion  groups, and workshops. She is most excited when her clients eliminate toxic emotional residue and limiting beliefs that have held them back, freeing them up for the life, performance, and success that God has planned. You can reach Cresenda at cresenda@cresendajones.com.

ILLUMINATION PUBLISHERS

www.ipibooks.com

Contents

Acknowledgments

Most of all, I appreciate and thank God, the giver of all grace, hope, wisdom, knowledge, transformations, and growth. With God, all things are possible—spiritual transformation and maturity, emotional intelligence, and emotional freedom! Apart from God, I can do nothing (John 15:5).

Secondly, no words could ever thank Simone Bell, who read every chapter, suggested edits, and provided constant encouragement. She knows my love language—acts of service. Thank you for your love for me and your unwavering faith in God and in me! My brother in Christ, Michael Burns, voluntarily went above and beyond by reading to provide feedback. He encouraged my soul! Amy Morgan and Gina Poirier likewise have been an angels of encouragement. A special thanks also goes out to those who read a portion of the workbook and provided feedback: Mark and Kenda Moloney, Lindy Jurado, Jeanie Shaw, Monica Alvarez, Natalie Ludewig, Beverly Ozanne, Natacha Pierre, Kynita Smalls, Octavia Lloyd-Oliver, Tina Kelly, and Monica Edwards. I am grateful for your investment of time and love! I am so very grateful for Derek Canton, who has become one of my closest friends and brings much joy to my life. I feel blessed beyond measure that God connected us. Thanks also to my family members Vernon Jones (dec), Joyce Siler, Carmen Jones, and Dewayne Jones, who have shown love and care, and who have given their best.

A special thanks to Dr. Timothy Sumerlin, founder of Disciples In Motion, who has been an example and encouragement in his own work to support brothers and sisters all over the world. I appreciate his willingness to write the foreword to this workbook. Despite his international reach, he makes an effort to see and support each of us individually. This reminds me of Jesus and how people in His presence felt loved. I also feel the same about my "brother from another mother," Paul Vasquez. His family, encouragement, and friendship have been an inexplicable inspiration, support, and joy.

Lastly, I want to thank my heroes and partners in personal, character, spiritual, and emotional growth. *The Healing for Damaged Emotions Workbook* discussion group participants in Philadelphia, South Jersey, Central Jersey, North Jersey, the Bronx, Brooklyn, Miami, and Palm Beach are my heroes. These men and women pushed past their fears to deal with emotional health issues. Such a journey takes immense courage. You all have given me wind for my wings! Participants in Mastering Emotional Intelligence® workshops have also been inspirations. Most recently, coaching clients who have completed the Time Line Therapy® breakthrough process, taken radical and relentless action, and focused on creating the future they desire have fueled my passion to transform our world! Thank you!

Dedication

This book is dedicated to my dear mother, Joyce Siler. She is now an 80-year-old disciple of Christ in Philadelphia, Pennsylvania. We have become closer than ever as we increasingly accept ourselves and each other in addition to more vulnerably sharing our hearts. After enduring a very challenging childhood in America's 1940s and 1950s, my mom modeled courage when she accepted the invitation to study the Bible (in 1985) in a fellowship that strove to not only know the Bible but to make it their focus to do what the Bible says.

Mom then, in her 50s, after a time of prodding and persuasion, was willing to focus on her own personal healing and growth with the support of a professional therapist. With both of these courageous actions and with her lifetime of empathy, care, and advocacy for others, I am so very grateful and proud to be her daughter and sister in Christ! My prayer is that through this workbook I will pass on some of the love, knowledge, richness, and transformation tools that my mom models. It has been one of my greatest joys to have Mom as a partner in the gospel!

Foreword

A kindred spirit is a rare find. I found one in Cresenda Jones. We connected the first time we met. Wise, full of passion, cheerful, intelligent, and possessing a unique sense of humor, Cresenda has a hunger to help those seeking change. She is a wonderful example of the connections that take place with good emotional intelligence and is the perfect writer for this project.

Moreover, Cresenda has a kindred spirit in Jesus. You see, Jesus is all about connecting with others. We see it throughout the Scriptures. He connected with the blind, the paralytics, the bleeding woman, the disciples, and on and on. Some in their amazement remarked, "He has done everything well" (Mark 7:37). Indeed he has. First, He knew himself, "that he had come from God and was returning to God" (John 13:3). And He knew in His spirit what people were thinking (Matthew 12:25), what was in their hearts (Matthew 9:4), and how to respond in amazing and astonishing ways that transformed those who spent time with Him. That is what emotional intelligence is all about: knowing yourself in such a way that you can recognize and manage your own emotional makeup, thus enabling you to connect to others in meaningful ways that bring about change—like Jesus.

In the spirit of Jesus, the Apostle Paul called disciples to "become all things to all people" (1 Corinthians 9:22). A tall order? You bet. These kinds of changes do not come easily. Cresenda will make you work to develop these essential skills. She will skillfully lead you through exciting new learning and a variety of exercises and challenges. You will grow to better know and be aware of yourself and how to manage your emotions. This will allow you to better understand and connect with others. This vital ability will increase your capacity to manage difficult and complex social situations, which will always be a part of the church environment.

In Cresenda's previous book, *Spiritual Maturity: God's Will for Emotional Health and Healing* (2014), she dives into our emotional world and explains how God not only designed us for emotions, but also how he wants to connect with us through those emotions. She states, "Either we know, understand, and manage our emotions, or they control us. In order to be healthy spiritually and emotionally, we must know ourselves." Cresenda acts as a guide for the reader to continue their journey to a healthy emotional maturity that can in turn benefit others. As she explains, this workbook provides "a roadmap for our desired goals and outcomes—

increased spiritual maturity along with emotional intelligence and freedom! Let's continue the journey!"

Indeed, spiritual maturity and relationships are our life—they are some of our highest priorities. May you enjoy the journey and be blessed by it, as I was.

—Dr. Timothy Sumerlin
Author of *The Grief Journey: Finding Peace in All of Life's Losses and Recovery Moving Forward,* www.inmotioncounseling.org.
Denver, 2021

Introduction

People will forget what you said and what you did, but they will never forget how you made them feel.
—Maya Angelou

For you created my inmost being;
you knit me together in my mother's womb.
—Psalm 139:13

In September 2018, we started the first Men of Freedom discussion group in Miami, Florida. The men came committed to studying and discussing David Seamands' *Healing for Damaged Emotions Workbook*. I had been privileged to facilitate 12 groups of women who discussed this life-changing workbook. This would be the first group of men! During one of our meetings we discussed and made a list of the characteristics of people who either brought out the best in us or the worst in us. The men were asked to picture a person in their mind and to think about that individual's characteristics. We came up with a list of descriptions for both categories.

Those who brought out the *best* in us were:

Thoughtful	Loving/Loveable	Encouraging	Giving
God-fearing	Accountable	Caring	Available
Loving	Resilient	Considerate	Joyful
Generous	Forgiving	Understanding	Funny
Assertive	Courageous	Kind	Confident
Supportive	Vulnerable	Sacrificial	Inquisitive
Disciplined	Visionary	Hopeful	Curious
Merciful	Investing	Full of Integrity	Honest
Gracious	Patient	A Listener	
Inspiring	Awesome	Calm	

Those who brought out the *worst* in us were:

A Leech	Foolish	Manipulative	Mocking
Annoying	Overbearing	Nasty	Mean
Selfish	Selfish	Angry	Vulgar
Greedy	Arrogant	Insensitive	Insecure
Accosting	Deceitful	Draining	Abusive
Exasperating	Slimy	Hurt/Hurtful	Violent

As disciples, the foundation for all that we do is our relationship with God. With that in mind, the men in the group not only provided words that describe spiritual health, they also provided words that describe practical people skills. In essence, they described emotional intelligence (EQ). EQ, as defined by Daniel Goleman (1995), *is the ability to know and manage one's own feelings well and to read and deal with others' emotions well.*

God has called us to love deeply (1 Corinthians 13:1–13) and to allow the fruit of the Spirit (Galatians 5:22–26) to become ubiquitous in our lives. We know about the refreshing (Acts 3:19) and full life of godliness, love, and holiness that we are called to, referred to as life "to the full" in John 10:10. God truly has planned the absolute best life for us. He desires that we become intimately close to Him—spiritually mature. God desires that we also have amazing relationships—the essence of EQ. "No good thing does he withhold from those whose walk is blameless" (Psalm 84:11). Yet many of us have had a hard time figuring out how to actualize all the amazing things that God has planned for us. The question is, HOW do we realize God's plan for spiritual transformation and emotional intelligence in our personal lives? It is the goal of this workbook to provide a roadmap for our desired goals and outcomes—increased spiritual maturity along with emotional intelligence and freedom! Let's continue the journey!

In the worlds of science, business, and academics, IQ is no longer considered the sole measure of human aptitudes. Goleman (1995) reports that, "IQ contributes about 20 percent to the factors that determine life success, which leaves 80 percent to other forces" (p. 34). Though there is intersection, academic intelligence, dutifulness, and even Bible knowledge will not lead us to our desired success, performance, and outcomes unless attention is also given to our emotional lives. We all have seen people whom we have considered highly intelligent and even "spiritual" do extremely emotional and irrational things. I can certainly give examples from my own life, which I will share! Saul exemplified this principle in 1

Samuel 15 when he did not obey God regarding the Amalekites. In verse 24 of the chapter, Saul's lack of EQ—"I was afraid...and so I gave in to them"—resulted in his rejection as king. James 1:2–4 also calls us to be "mature and well-developed, not deficient in any way" (MSG). People with high levels of EQ (personal and social competence) have been found to be more successful, content, productive, clear in thought, focused, and more advantaged in multiple domains of life (Goleman, 1995). EQ has been the missing link on many a journey to spiritual maturity. In addition, we have started to understand that we can only be spiritually mature when we are emotionally mature (Scazzerro, 2003). We must ensure that we do not miss the emotional intelligence link in our spiritual transformation efforts and our maturing process!

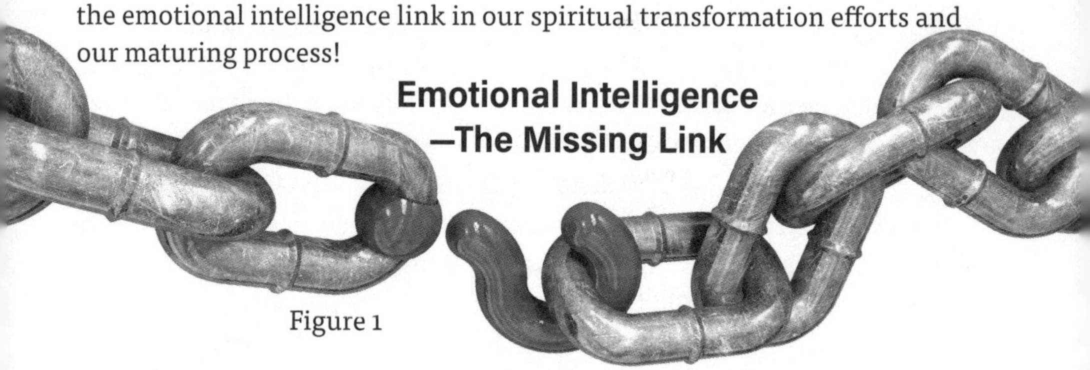

Emotional Intelligence —The Missing Link

Figure 1

Bradberry and Greaves (2009) found that only 36 percent of people assessed "are able to accurately identify their emotions as they happen" (p. 14). They also note that "EQ is the foundation for a host of critical skills" (p. 20) such as decision-making, change tolerance, communication, customer service, flexibility, accountability, social skills, trust, anger management, stress tolerance, presentation skills, empathy, time management, and assertiveness. I am sure that you can imagine or picture someone who knows and can quote scriptures, but whose life does not resemble the list of "those who brought out the best in us" that the Men of Freedom group provided. That is the heartbreaking news. EQ is the missing link for many, as represented by the question mark in the chain links (Figure 1). The great news is that intentional effort spent on increasing our EQ tends to have a wide-ranging, positive impact on our lives. Bradberry and Greaves also note that "EQ is so critical to success that it accounts for 58 percent of performance in all types of jobs" (p. 20). They also found that there is a direct link between EQ and annual salaries. They note that in the context of work, 90 percent of high performers are also high in EQ, but only 20 percent of low performers are high in EQ.

Please take a careful look again at the list of the characteristics of those who brought out the best and worst in the Men of Freedom discussion group participants.

1. Which list would your close friends and family say your life most resembles?

2. Which of the two lists would you say most resembles your life?

3. Which of the two lists would God say most resembles your life?

The brothers in the Men of Freedom group described EQ well when they discussed those who were able to bring out the best in them. We can all think of Christians/disciples who are committed to living godly lives, to reading their Bibles, praying, evangelizing, serving, and all—yet those same individuals struggle to reach their full potential (see John 10:10, 15:16). Many times, the missing link or blind spot is emotional intelligence—maturity and congruence with our heart, mind, soul, and strength.

For most of my life as a disciple of Christ, I have been working hard to reverse the generational dysfunction of ignoring emotions and denying realities in our family and the world. To this end, my prayer has been: "Create in me a pure heart, O God, and renew a steadfast spirit within me" (Psalm 51:10). Both my parents were emotionally unavailable. Neither of them had parents who allowed them to be human in regard to our God-given emotions. My dad was born in 1934 and my mom in 1939. Our society at the time was conflicted with how people of African descent were to be considered: either human beings or property to be used for profit and gruesome pleasures. Emotions overall were not considered, but especially acknowledging the emotions of people of color.

I distinctly remember the scene from the movie *The Butler* where the young boy witnessed the killing of his father (who had spoken up about the sexual abuse of the boy's mother). No one at the scene of the murder dared to say anything about this atrocity. Everyone was expected to continue to work in the fields as if nothing had happened. There was no processing or expression of emotions allowed. Not only were people of color not to have emotions, but they were not even allowed to speak of the terror they witnessed and endured on a daily basis. Think of the level of trauma the enslaved experienced each day. The decades of enslavement, Jim Crow laws, and mass incarceration here in the United States impacted not only the enslaved, but also those whose hearts were seared by their own sins of oppression, hate, greed, abuse, lust, and murder. These mores do not simply disappear. Our way of life becomes ingrained in our DNA and subconscious mind.

In *The Body Keeps the Score: Brain, Mind and Body in the Healing of Trauma,*

Bessel Van Der Kolk (2014) notes that traumatic experiences "leave traces on our minds and emotions, on our capacity for joy and intimacy, and even on our biology and immune systems. Trauma affects not only those who are directly exposed to it, but also those around them" (Prologue, paras. 2 & 3). More recently, the Centers for Disease Control and Prevention notes that:

> One in five Americans was sexually molested as a child; one in four was beaten by a parent to the point of a mark being left on their body; and one in three couples engages in physical violence. A quarter of us grew up with alcoholic relatives, and one out of eight witnessed their mother being beaten or hit.

Those percentages are harrowing. Trauma, anger, sadness, fear, hurt, and guilt, if not effectively processed, will lead to being emotionally stunted, frozen, or stuck. The goal of this workbook is to share the vital emotional intelligence research and information that can fuel our spiritual inspiration and catapult us to the next level in our hearts, minds, souls, lives, professions, performance, leadership, results, and relationships!

- If you struggle with insecurity, this book is for you.
- If you struggle with addictions and impurity, this book is for you.
- If your marriage is on the rocks, this book is for you.
- If you need tools to navigate the emotions of your children, this book is for you.
- If you have not been able to effectively manage or let go of inappropriate anger, sadness, fear, hurt, or guilt, this book is for you.
- If you have not been able to let go of negative tapes or limiting beliefs, this book is for you.
- If you are a single Christian male and cannot figure out why you are not married after 10+ years as a disciple, this book is for you.
- If you just cannot seem to do well in work situations, this book is for you.
- If you are insufficiently in touch with your emotions or those of your loved ones, this book is for you.
- If you are unsatisfactorily connecting at a heart level with those in your life, this book is for you.

- If you have trouble articulating how you feel, this book is for you.
- If you do not feel that you have permission to be a human being, rest, cry, and take care of yourself, this book is for you!
- If you have had health problems that the doctors can't seem to figure out, this book can be helpful for you.
- If you are feeling burned out, this book can help you.
- If you suffer from mental illness and you want to know more about a biblical approach to emotional wellness, this book is for you (as a supplement to a professional treatment plan).
- If you are in a spiritual community with anyone who would relate to or be described by the above statements, then this book is for you.

Emotional intelligence is the blind spot that causes many of the "fires" ministers must repeatedly attempt to put out. EQ is the missing link for many involved in restoration-of-purity ministries. EQ is the missing link for disciples who just can't seem to get unstuck in their lives. EQ, no matter how committed we are to spiritual disciplines, is imperative for our relationship with God, peak performance, and success. In addition, we need practical strategies—a roadmap—for improving our EQ skills.

To be spiritually mature, it is essential that we become emotionally mature in our inmost being. The biological, psychological, social, and spiritual components of our being are all connected and interdependent. Dan Allender (1994) aptly states that "the Psalms help us understand that every emotion is a theological statement" (p. 16). Therefore, as disciples we must understand emotional intelligence—our inmost being—and its impact on our relationships with God, ourselves, and others so that we can be transformed (Romans 12:2) and free.

The first section of this workbook will discuss emotional intelligence in depth. To set our goals, we will need to first understand where we are with regard to EQ. The EQ Appraisal® found in *Emotional Intelligence 2.0* is recommended as a baseline self-assessment activity. Life without EQ and the importance of EQ are described. Further descriptions of EQ and how important it is to understand our brain and the cost of repressing emotions are discussed.

In the second section of this workbook, we focus on God, the Bible, and EQ. We look at what God says about emotions in general, people's emotions, emotional intelligence, and we examine scriptures on the four components of EQ. We also dive into how we can build EQ skills with a discussion of 66 strategies. This includes how we can better manage emotions.

The last section of the book discusses further details about our conscious and subconscious minds and a powerful therapeutic technique, Time Line Therapy®, that eliminates the harmful emotional residue and limiting decisions connected to past events. The idea that we can transform our neurology or rewrite neural circuits is thrilling!

Just as educators, salespeople, politicians, and clinicians now understand that there are multiple intelligences (Goleman, 1995), spiritual leaders are beginning to understand that spiritual disciplines, without an intentional focus on EQ, will not lead to the personal/personality transformations and fruitfulness that God has planned for His beloved children. As EQ researchers and trainers have frequently noted, a major goal is to bring our intelligence to our emotions. Unfortunately for us, we have focused many times on spirituality without including our emotional intelligence. Spiritual disciplines are about taking care of our soul (psyche in Greek); we must be intentional about our focus on the deep waters (Proverbs 20:5) and being healthy emotionally.

We probably cannot imagine a world or a close relationship void of emotion. Imagine how much better our world and relationships can be if we become proficient in our emotional intelligence! Goleman (1995) notes that no intelligence is more important than interpersonal intelligence: "If you don't have it, you'll make poor choices about who to marry, what job to take, and so on" (p. 42). If we want to excel in the practicalities of life, we need emotional intelligence combined with spiritual maturity! We need this EQ "missing link." "To love and to work, Sigmund Freud once remarked to his disciple Erik Erikson, are the twin capacities that mark full maturity" (Goleman, 1995, p. 129). It's ironic that Freud said that love is the full mark of maturity, since he was an atheist. Since God is love and has done amazing works, this is one thing He may possibly agree with Freud on.

> Jesus replied: "Love the Lord your God with all your heart and with all your soul and with all your mind." (Matthew 22:37)

> LORD Almighty, you...examine the righteous and probe the heart and mind. (Jeremiah 20:12)

God has called us to love Him with all our heart (the seat of our emotions) and mind (intelligence). This workbook will explore what

God says about EQ; what EQ is and its impact on our relationships with God, ourselves, and others; and how to build EQ skills. If we each work to master these skills, we can reach our full potential, help others to live for God, and live life to the full (John 10:10) as God has planned! This workbook provides the "missing link": the information that can build on and sustain the inspiration we consistently receive to love God with all our hearts and minds. This growth in EQ will allow us to glorify God with even more of our hearts and minds. As a result of working through this book and reflecting on the questions throughout, my prayer is that you will have more information/intelligence and tools for personal and relational transformation (Romans 12:2). Practicing the strategies for increasing EQ will greatly impact your individual, family, community, and church life. To God be the glory!

Since there is a wealth of scriptures in this workbook, a full list of the Scripture references and passages for each chapter are posted on my website (www.cresendajones.com).

Chapter One

Take the *Emotional Intelligence 2.0* test Assessment Is Imperative!

Examine yourselves...; test yourselves.
—2 Corinthians 13:5

Each one should test their own actions.
—Galatians 6:4

To continue our spiritual transformation journey, we need to know exactly where we are on the roadmap along the way. Whether it is regarding strategic planning, personal growth, planning for a class, planning to get healthier, improving financial status, or working to become more like Jesus, an assessment is imperative! There is little that compares to the gamut of emotions we experience while preparing for an assessment, expecting the test results, and then getting those results. For example, when waiting for results from a medical test that determines if we or a loved one has cancer, we become much more aware of the multitude of emotions flooding our world. Or for some, it is waiting for college entrance examination results— you are aware of the preparation that took place before the exam, followed by the hope that your score will be high enough to usher you into the college or university of your choice. And then there are those of you who have tried and waited for years for a successful pregnancy. After taking the test, you may be filled with excitement, fright, anxiety, hope, and intense prayers while waiting for the results. Or maybe you have studied for a career-related licensing or certification test and have the following sentiment I have heard from several folks: "I just can't wait to get this over with!" With the results from all these tests, we are able to understand exactly where we stand medically, academically, or vocationally. Then we have the information required to identify our strengths and areas in need of attention, and to plan next steps. None of us would allow a doctor to prescribe medications or a treatment plan without first checking all vitals and doing a thorough physical examination.

We learn from the Scriptures that God examines us (Psalms 11:4, 17:3,

26:2), and as committed disciples of Christ, we are called to do the same; to be sober minded (1 Peter 5:8, 1:13, 4:7; Romans 12:3; 1 Thessalonians 5:6, 8) and to test ourselves (2 Corinthians 13:5). Yes, completing an assessment is imperative!

It is the same with spiritual maturity and emotional intelligence. Yet many of us are not aware of what EQ is, or how we can develop a plan to improve our EQ skills of self-awareness, self-control/management, social awareness, and relationship management. All of these skills are important to God and to our ability to live the fruitful life to the full that He has planned for us, as seen in John 15 and John 10:10. Even more telling—and challenging—are Jesus' statements that a good tree cannot bear bad fruit, a bad tree cannot bear good fruit, and every tree that does not bear good fruit is cut down and thrown into the fire (Matthew 7:18–19). It is to our Father's glory that we bear much fruit, showing ourselves to be His disciples (John 15:8). We have been chosen and appointed to go and bear fruit, fruit that will last (John 15:16). This requires all the skills of EQ. We have all encountered people with little self-awareness, social awareness, self-control, and social/ relationship skills, which is not mentioned in a negative or judgmental way here, just as a matter of observance. Remember, we all need grace. But without these skills, it is challenging to bear fruit that lasts or live lives of maximum success.

Many Christians/disciples have taken the appraisal offered in *Emotional Intelligence 2.0* (Bradberry & Graves, 2009). This book reinforces some of the most encouraging news that science has provided about EQ, which is that our brain has the ability to change. Neurologists, biologists, and researchers have informed us that we have neuroplasticity. Our brains can develop the new connections (also known as neural circuits) we need in order to develop greater EQ skills. This is indeed good news for you and me!

God has continued to graciously show me that these skills that were not developed in my formative years must continually be an intentional focus. Many disciples and friends have patiently persevered through all my EQ-challenged moments. If I were bowling or playing golf, a handicap would likely be needed. Yet, as Paul writes in 1 Corinthians 1:5, God has enriched us in every way—with all kinds of speech and with all knowledge. Amen that despite our deficits, God gives us the power and resources for the transformation mentioned in Romans 12:2! Paul declared, "And we all, who with unveiled faces contemplate the Lord's glory, are being transformed into his image with ever-increasing glory, which comes from the Lord, who is the Spirit" (2 Corinthians 3:18).

If you do not have the book *Emotional Intelligence 2.0* (Bradberry & Greaves, 2009) and have not taken the appraisal, **I encourage you now to purchase the book** (it is available instantly as an ebook or wherever books are sold) **and take the assessment right away.** The appraisal only takes 7–10 minutes to complete so that you can obtain potentially transformative information. Please record your scores in the chart in the *"My Emotional Intelligence Appraisal®* Scores" column.

Emotional Intelligence 2.0 Assessment Result	Average (out of 100)	My *Emotional Intelligence Appraisal®* Scores
Overall EQ score	68	
Personal competence	68	
Self-awareness	68	
Self-management	67	
Social competence	70	
Social awareness	69	
Relationship management	68	

The second column is a compilation of the results from over forty appraisals of disciples who have participated in EQ workshops. With baseline EQ information, as Bradberry & Greaves note in Chapter 4 of their book, you will a) be able to understand where your strengths and areas in need of attention are; b) pick an EQ skill to work on; c) pick strategies to use for the development of your chosen EQ skill; d) share your goals with a mentor; e) practice, practice, practice; and f) measure your progress.

Over the years, I have continued to work on my EQ skills and have participated in the TalentSmart® seminar where individuals are trained to facilitate the "Mastering Emotional Intelligence" workshop. This powerful workshop is my favorite to facilitate. I also completed the EQ Multi-Rater (360º) Edition assessment where 10 friends and coworkers anonymously provided feedback on my EQ skill level. With the 2012 appraisal, my overall EQ score, as I rated myself, was 79. Notably, my average EQ score as rated by others was 73. It was an eye-opening experience. What is truly fun is that the 34-page results report includes 17 EQ lessons (using memorable movie clips) that individually help us to increase our understanding of and capacity for each EQ skill. This work has been a journey. My journey continues.

As alluded to above, TalentSmart® offers several assessments, but this EQ appraisal is wonderful as a starting point for understanding our personal skill levels. The 28 skill (not behavioral) items on the assessment evaluate self-awareness, self-management, social awareness, and relationship management skills. Since the developers are researchers, they have considered both reliability and validity. The appraisal drills down to specifics, and results are tied to three recommended strategies in the *Emotional Intelligence 2.0* book. TalentSmart® also offers online EQ lessons and goal tracking. Those who take the appraisal will even be able to set a reminder for retesting their EQ at a later date. I personally have taken the assessment about five times. Though my scores have fluctuated some, it was great to go back and review my scores from when I first took the appraisal in 2010. At the time, my overall EQ score was 80. One of my lowest scores was in 2012, when I had an overall EQ score of 67.

What Do the *Emotional Intelligence Appraisal®* Scores Mean?

In your TalentSmart® *Emotional Intelligence Appraisal®* results report, Bradberry & Greaves (2009) share what the EQ *Appraisal®* scores mean about your current skill level based on a normed sample.

90–100	A strength to capitalize on
80–89	A strength to build on
70–79	With a little improvement, this could be a strength
60–69	Something you should work on
59 and below	A concern you must address

Reflection:
How do you feel about your scores?

_____

_____

What do you think about your scores?

_____

_____

Which of the EQ skills (self-awareness, self-management, social awareness, relationship management) is your strength (found on the "What the Scores Mean" results page)?

_____

Which of the EQ skills is something to work on or what brings your score down the most?

_____

Which three strategies (one per month) will you work on first—as noted in your results (page 4)?

Month: _____   Strategy: _____

Month: _____   Strategy: _____

Month: _____   Strategy: _____

Who can you check in with on a weekly basis regarding your progress?

_____

How can you intentionally be cognizant of and implement this month's strategy in your daily life?

_____

_____

_____

I typically joke and say that I spent $7,000 to be trained to facilitate the Mastering Emotional Intelligence® workshop, and what I learned as the most helpful EQ strategy for me was that I need to "Breathe Right" in order to increase my self-management skills. This is an ironic strategy/directive, as when I moved back to New Jersey from Florida in February 2019 to look after my mom (Alzheimer's diagnosis), I was diagnosed with asthma. I had major breathing issues and was instructed to take four prescriptions and weekly allergy shots. I felt that my brain was just not working correctly. Lo and behold, the "Breathe Right" self-management strategy notes that when we "choose to breathe right," we "flood our brain with oxygen" and can "notice the effects immediately" (Bradberry & Greaves, p. 102). A calmer, relaxed, and clearheaded mental and emotional state of mind is what I felt I was missing when I moved back to New Jersey. I was not able to process things well. My rational brain was not fueled with the needed oxygen and power.

As always, God worked. I researched pollution and pollen, and I found an area in Florida that has better air quality, so I moved back. My brain, and thus my quality of life, depends on it! Research study after research study has informed us that EQ has a major impact on our ability to be successful.

With an understanding of where we stand with regard to our EQ skills, we can make a more effective effort to develop our personal strategic plan for increasing our EQ. If you are unable to purchase Bradberry and Greaves' *Emotional Intelligence 2.0*, there are a number of free EQ assessments online. Links for free online assessments can be found on my website at www.cresendajones.com.

> *For this very reason, make every effort to add to your faith goodness; and to goodness, knowledge; and to knowledge, self-control; and to self-control, perseverance; and to perseverance, godliness; and to godliness, mutual affection; and to mutual affection, love. For if you possess these qualities in increasing measure, they will keep you from being ineffective and unproductive in your knowledge of our Lord Jesus Christ.* (2 Peter 1:5–8)

Chapter One Summary

To internalize the information you have read and reflected upon, please select the **three main points** that resonated with you.

To anchor your **top three learnings** or (new or deepened) convictions, list them here:

_____

_____

_____

_____

_____

You can more thoroughly anchor your learnings by making at least one decision on how to implement what you've learned. If your decision can be written in the SMART (Specific, Measurable, Attainable/Achievable, Relevant, and Timed) format, you will have a better chance of it becoming a reality! Record your **one SMART decision** here:

_____

_____

_____

_____

_____

_____

God, Growth & EQ—Natacha's Testimony

I participated in a mini workshop on emotional intelligence through a singles retreat at my local church about three years ago. At that time, I learned more about emotional intelligence and that we have the ability to change and grow for God, ourselves, and all those He puts in our lives. I have always been attracted to investing in myself to grow and mature personally and spiritually. I took the assessment that scored me in four different emotional areas (self-awareness, self-management, social awareness, and relationship management). My initial scores indicated that I was aware of "some" behaviors and doing them well, but that there were other behaviors holding me back. *Emotional intelligence 2.0* mentions that most people start here and that with increased awareness, we have the opportunity to improve in the weaker areas. For me, this was exciting. I felt very hopeful that through this book and assessment, I had tools and strategies for how to improve. Knowing and having awareness is only half the battle; we also need the strategies on how to act and improve on what we know.

Emotional Intelligence 2.0 was keen on providing the "how" to deal with areas that needed strengthening. I love that just by applying new behaviors I was able to improve my awareness of myself and increase my management of these areas. Three years later, with additional tools and an ongoing desire to be better for God, I retook the test and saw improvements in my results. My second test revealed above-average results, with a few areas that still needed attention. Overall, this growth reflected the things that, with God's help, I was able to do well. It also reflected that with continued practice and study of my behaviors I could polish my skills even more. I often think about what a thriving, full, abundant life looks like. I also like to ask myself if that is the state I am living and growing in—or am I far from it?

Answering that question requires having a sober estimate of myself. Taking this assessment was one way to have the indicators I needed to see the things I could act on to make any changes that were needed. I love that part of growing in these areas also required input from safe, trusted people that could provide valid insight into character issues and emotional and spiritual challenges. Who I am today is a result of the collective work of being in God's kingdom. As a result of my community of healthy relationships and access to resources and tools, I can experience all that God wants me to be and have. Doing the work is not often easy; it requires intention, a deliberate will to accept what is and the willingness to make the changes that are needed. I am incredibly grateful for God's continued help and His abundant resources to continue to mature, grow, and become my best for Christ.

My life scripture, John 10:10, tells me that the thief comes only to steal and kill and destroy and that Jesus came that we may have life, and have it to the full. For me, God has paid too high a price for me not to have a thriving life. Having poor emotional and spiritual health will steal, kill, and destroy everything that God came to offer me. For me to truly embrace having a thriving and abundant life requires that I make the most of growing in areas that hinder me from being my best in this world. If God thought it was important enough to send His Son to endure all that He did to offer me a shot at an AMAZING life, I ought to consider doing my part to experience what that life, which He paid an incredible debt for, could look like for me. It is a call to excellence, to growth, and to a growing faith. This does not just happen without increasing awareness and doing the practical work to implement the change we want to experience.

Chapter Two

Life without EQ

When the student is ready, the teacher will appear.
—Lao Tzu

Brothers and sisters, I could not address you as people who live by the Spirit but as people who are still worldly—mere infants in Christ. I gave you milk, not solid food, for you were not yet ready for it. Indeed, you are still not ready. You are still worldly. For since there is jealousy and quarreling among you, are you not worldly? Are you not acting like mere humans?
—1 Corinthians 3:1–5

The acts of the flesh are obvious: sexual immorality, impurity and debauchery; idolatry and witchcraft; hatred, discord, jealousy, fits of rage, selfish ambition, dissensions, factions and envy; drunkenness, orgies, and the like. I warn you, as I did before, that those who live like this will not inherit the kingdom of God.
—Galatians 5:19–21

So then let us not sleep [in spiritual indifference] as the rest [of the world does], but let us keep wide awake [alert and cautious] and let us be sober [self-controlled, calm, and wise].
—1 Thessalonians 5:6 (AMP)

I hope that you have downloaded or purchased *Emotional Intelligence 2.0* (2009) and taken the assessment. Bradberry and Graves (2009) do an excellent job describing how people with low EQ scores manage their emotions and interact with others in the workplace, which can be extrapolated to cover interactions outside work. You can learn a lot about yourself, your loved ones, and those you work with through the EQ Appraisal®, its results, and the video lessons.

In the context discipleship and our walk with God in the fellowship, I am sure that if you are plugged in and connected to even a few others, you are aware of the challenges in our personal levels of the four EQ skills—self-awareness, self-management, social awareness, and relationship management. For many, these challenges were present before becoming disciples. For some, they continue to cause significant distress or impairment over time.

I recall partnering with a group who cared about the education of children to work toward opening a private high school that could meet the needs of the underserved in Philadelphia. Unfortunately, after one year, we had to close the school due to lack of funds. Later, I had a conversation with one of our church leaders, who noted that the students enrolled in the school were from some of the most "challenged" families in our fellowship. I thought, *Wow, I wish I had been aware of that context while I was dealing with all the related and highly intense issues that surfaced.* My level of awareness at the time was not sharp enough to see the forest while I was on the front line feeling lost among the trees. My self- and social awareness EQ skills definitely were not sufficient.

In addition, my dear friend and fellow full-time worker at the school mentioned that I seemed to need to control everything. At the time, I didn't see how my hypervigilance, perfectionism, and low self-esteem led me to indefatigable striving in countless unhealthy ways. My EQ was way too low. I am extremely grateful that God had a plan for me to focus on my own personal growth through the support of disciples, mentors, coaches, and professional therapists. I clearly see that God has continually led me to competent teachers (possessing awareness, knowledge, and skills) who have provided the information and safe places for my personal growth and development. I'm guessing that we all can relate to personal challenges and the challenges we see in relationships around us.

The Men of Freedom discussion group in Miami, Florida (as mentioned in the introduction) also described people with low EQ. After thinking about who it would be and picturing that person in their mind, they came up with a list of characteristics of those who brought out the worst in them. We do not perform optimally when working with people who bring out the worst in us.

Those who brought out the *worst* in us were:

A Leech	Foolish	Manipulative	Mocking
Annoying	Overbearing	Nasty	Mean
Selfish	Abusive	Angry	Vulgar
Greedy	Arrogant	Insensitive	Insecure
Accosting	Deceitful	Draining	Violent
Exasperating	Slimy	Hurt/Hurtful	

Reflection:
When you think of a person (picture them in your mind) who brought out the worst in you, what additional characteristics would you include?

_____

_____

_____

I'm sure you have also personally felt or at least seen the difficulties related to insufficient EQ skills. Those with low EQ can be described as people who:

- Are exasperated with their own and others' emotions
- Do not understand or consider the emotions of others
- Feel that they just can't get/feel close to God or others
- May have high IQ, but do not get along with, work well with, or maintain friendships with others
- Do not listen, especially to the viewpoints of others
- Blame others or do not take responsibility for problems
- Have emotional outbursts or erratic behavior
- Lack empathy
- Frequently get in arguments/disputes/conflicts
- Exhibit inappropriate responses
- Have major problems at work, in school, or with family, friendships, or romantic relationships
- Don't feel that they have good relationships, unity or "family feeling" with others
- Are not aware of their impact (through words /actions) on others
- Are not aware of why they are having continued and repeated relationship difficulties
- Are not adept with stress management, critical thinking, change tolerance, decision-making, time management, teamwork, or communication.

Though we can typically witness the lack of EQ skills in social and work relationships, it is always fun to facilitate a Mastering EQ workshop where we look at a few movie clips and discuss the presence or lack of EQ skills.

TalentSmart® (www.talentsmart.com) has also published video clips and helpful commentaries of the Top Ten Emotional Intelligence Moments for several years. They are priceless and entertaining.

Life with Insufficient Self-Awareness

When we are not aware of our emotions as they happen, we are at their mercy. We can be uneasy with human sexuality or internalize anger, which can turn into depression, guilt, and shame. When we do not allow ourselves to be in touch with our emotions, we can become aggressive or passive instead of assertive. We will likely have low self-esteem and an unhealthy self-concept. An individual with low self-awareness would likely not be comfortable enough to be spontaneous or playful, as ruminations and obsessions may be prevalent. Without mindful awareness, one can become engulfed or lost in emotions and feel overwhelmed and powerless in efforts for spirituality and self-discipline. A person without self-awareness will likely feel that they have no control over their emotions.

Goleman (1995) compared the different ways that we can attend to and deal with our emotions. He compares those who are self-aware with those who are engulfed or accepting. Self-awareness is the goal, and as a preview to the chapter on the three requisites for change, Goleman (1995) notes that those who accept their emotions and decide not to act to change them can become resigned to depression or other unwarranted emotions. If we experience emotions as overwhelming or distressful, we may work to avoid feeling much at all. When we do not have sufficient self-awareness, we moreover can experience emotional distress through physical or somatic symptoms. When we are not aware of our feelings, it will be impossible to articulate them, let alone to manage them effectively.

Those with low self-awareness are also likely to have limited emotional vocabulary, have trouble discriminating between various emotions, and not know or lack any sense of what they are feeling. They can be oblivious to feelings about events or emotionally flat or numb. Joann Love (2016) noted five warning signs of a lack of self-awareness: being constantly defensive, micromanaging, making excuses, being accused of being a bully, and living in denial.

Since emotions impact all our choices, those without self-awareness may have a difficult time making decisions. Reason without feeling can make us blind (Goleman, 1995). Goleman notes that "the key to sounder personal decision-making [is], in short: being attuned to our feelings" (p. 54). Without self-awareness, we are on a path to self-destruction (1 John 1:6–8).

Reflection:
Which lack of self-awareness descriptions fit you?

_____

_____

_____

Life with Insufficient Self-Management or Self-Control

One without sufficient self-management skills will constantly battle distress (Goleman, 1995), lower productivity, and ineffectiveness. Without self-control, one's anxiety, depression, and sexual urges can paralyze and defeat them. Resilience would also be deficient. Controlled by feelings of anger, sadness, fear, worried rumination, guilt/shame and hurt, one would be unpredictable, impulsive, and insensitive. Without the EQ skill of self-management, emotions can become highly inappropriate and unwarranted. One would likely be rash with emotional outbursts and a slave to emotions and passions (Romans 6:16, 20). We can also see evidence of a possible lack of self-control when one has compulsive spending or borrowing, underachieves at school or work, procrastinates, eats in unhealthy ways, or is not physically fit. A lack of self-control can correlate with or cause trauma. It should be noted that self-control must address not only our behavior, but also the impulses and emotions that fuel our behavior.

Scientifically, a lack of self-control has been shown to be a precursor to crime and drug use. In the *Journal of Behavioral Health Services & Research*, Conner, Stein, and Longshore (2009) note that low self-control has six subdomains: impulsiveness, preference for physical activities, risk seeking, self-centeredness, preference for simple tasks, and volatile temper. Social science research of this type has been used to develop interventions for offenders. When we add practical and godly interventions, we can easily reduce the risk of becoming offenders.

Spiritually, a lack of self-control has detrimental effects on our relationship with God, our relationship with ourselves, and our relationships with others. Proverbs 25:28 tells us that a person who lacks self-control is like a city whose walls are broken through. As we know, the walls around a city, in biblical days, were the inhabitants' protection. In addition, in Proverbs 16:32, it is amazing that God finds more value in us having patience and self-control than in us being warriors who conquer cities. In James 1:20 we are informed that "human anger does not produce the righteousness that God desires." Unfortunately, many of us did not have role models who handled anger well. Partly as a result of that, it seems, many Christians unconsciously feel that any and all anger is sin.

God has called us to be love and light. Biblically, self-control deals with our hearts and minds. The Bible discusses sober mindedness in 1 Timothy 3:2; Titus 1:8 and 2:2; and 1 Peter 4:7. Paul even discussed being in his right mind in 2 Corinthians 5:13 and Acts 26:25. We are all encouraged to have sober judgment and to not think of ourselves more highly than we ought (Romans 12:3). Paul also included a great description of a life lacking self-control in Romans 7.

God similarly implores us to resist the darkness. He calls us to strictly discipline our body in 1 Corinthians 9:25–27, to not behave in the passion of lust in 1 Thessalonians 4:3–5, and to make sure that we don't burn with passion in 1 Corinthians 7:9. Even more so, we can live self-controlled, upright, and godly lives in our present age (Titus 2:11–12). Among our goals as Christians, we strive to live with Jesus Christ as Lord and allow the love of Christ to control us (2 Corinthians 5:14).

> Be sober [well balanced and self-disciplined], be alert and cautious at all times. That enemy of yours, the devil, prowls around like a roaring lion [fiercely hungry], seeking someone to devour. (1 Peter 5:8 [AMP])

Reflection:

How have you seen a lack of self-control affect your life or that of those around you?

_____

_____

_____

Life with Insufficient Social Awareness Skills

Those without sufficient skills to connect with others typically cannot read other people's emotions. A lack of empathy precludes us from understanding what others need and want (Goleman, 1995). Those with a lack of social awareness can feel uncomfortable reaching out to new people. I have heard, countless times, the erroneous conflation of being an introvert with the lack of social intelligence. We can improve our EQ skills, and my hope is that introverts will not get a bad name because of those who are not willing to develop their social intelligence skills.

It is also difficult for one without social awareness to have effective interpersonal skills. When we lack social awareness, we tend to have deficits in sensitivity, insight, and communication ability. Organizational awareness and service orientation are also difficult. We can have difficulty understanding organizational culture, getting things done within an organization, and using informal processes and procedures in an organization. Some with low social awareness skills have difficulty helping others develop and also have difficulty using questioning skills to better understand issues.

Life with Insufficient Relationship Management Skills

I have often heard the dismay of disciples, including leaders, with regard to people who are struggling spiritually and relationally. We all want to do everything we can to strengthen our sisters and brothers in Christ. Many times, a lack of social competence is conflated with a lack of "spirituality." A lack of interpersonal effectiveness leaves people feeling isolated, insecure, and at the mercy of Satan, who is the roaring lion looking for someone to devour (1 Peter 5:8). As we know, isolation is one of Satan's schemes. Those with inadequate relationship management skills are not "comfortable with themselves, others, and the social universe they live in" (Goleman, 1995, p. 45). Without relationship management skills, one would have difficulty with communication, influencing others, conflict management, any type of leadership responsibility, building bonds, developing others, being a change catalyst, and teamwork and collaboration.

Independent of our IQ, we can be inept in our personal world. Our levels of EQ vary, and even vary within the four components that make up personal and social competence. Some of us who have intense struggles even wish that we didn't have emotions, passions, struggles, or human feelings. Yet EQ is what makes us human. God wants our heart, our passions, our soul—all of us (Mark 12:30)! In reference to our work lives, Daniel Goleman (1995) noted that executives are hired for their IQ, but fired for their lack of EQ. If someone brings out the worst in those around them, they would likely be fired from a job. So EQ determines our relationship and work success. Not only does a lack of EQ gravely impact our personal lives, but as the Men of Freedom group's list shows, a lack of EQ can negatively affect the people around us. In contrast, Jesus was excellent in everything. Therefore, we can be excellent and competent in emotional acuity.

Spiritually, God provides multiple examples of people living without self-awareness, self-control, social awareness, and healthy relationships. In 1 Corinthians 3, Paul referred to the people in that fellowship as carnal. Galatians 5:15 warns that relationship management skills can be overtaken by biting and devouring. Each time Bible letter recipients "grieved (Ephesians 4:30), quenched (1 Thessalonians 5:19), lied to (Acts 5:4), put to the test (Acts 5:9), insulted/outraged (Hebrews 10:29), made jealous (James 4:5), blasphemed (Matthew 12:31) and resisted (Acts 7:51)" (Edmiston, 2001, p. 40) the Holy Spirit or were devoid of the Spirit (Jude 1:19), we can see the opposite of spiritual maturity and emotional intelligence. Anytime we go against God's word, we will be negatively impacted spiritually and emotionally, which is the opposite of what God desires for us all.

With an understanding of and a picture of life without EQ, we can see why it is so important. God calls us to live a life of love (1 Corinthians 13:4–13) and to be filled with His Spirit (Galatians 5:22–23). The good news is that, unlike IQ, the skills of EQ can be developed! With higher EQ, research has shown that we can have better results in relationships, marriages, parenting, leadership, sales, earnings, health, productivity, and academics.

Reflection:

The Bible shares countless examples of believers and nonbelievers with insufficient EQ skills—self-awareness, self-control, social awareness, and healthy relationships. For example, in 1 Corinthians 3, Paul referred to the members of that group as carnal. In Galatians 5:15, Paul warned that their relationship management skills were at risk of being overtaken by biting and devouring one another. What additional examples come to mind?

_____

_____

_____

_____

_____

_____

_____ Chapter Two Summary _____

GREAT job working through this chapter. In order to internalize the information you have read and reflected upon, please select the **three main points** that resonated with you.

To anchor your **top three learnings** or (new or deepened) convictions, list them on the following lines:

_____

_____

_____

_____

You can thoroughly anchor your learnings by making at least one decision on how to implement what you've learned. If your decision can be written in the SMART (Specific, Measurable, Attainable/Achievable, Relevant, and Timed) format, you will have a better chance of it becoming a reality! Record your **one SMART decision** here:

_____

_____

_____

_____

_____

God, Marriage & EQ
Fernando and Rosa's Testimony

Proverbs 20:5 tells us that "the purposes of a person's heart are deep waters, but one who has insight draws them out." This, to us, exemplifies the importance of emotional intelligence. As a married couple, the importance of drawing out the deep purposes of our hearts is essential to understanding each other. It's amazing how even trivial conversations can devolve into conflicts because the needs of the heart are not being communicated or are being misunderstood.

For example, my wife may approach me with a simple question, "What are we doing for dinner tonight?" My response to that question is normally to think through what responsibilities I have that night and see what she has to do that night, what foods we have, and who prepares them better, etc. My wife, however, may really be thinking that she had a long day, is tired, and needs me to cook so she can lie down for a nap. In essence, she is not asking me what we are doing for dinner, she is asking me to cook so she can rest. Many couples reading this may be quite familiar with this dynamic! It's easy enough to think, "Why doesn't she just ask me to cook?" but the problem is that she feels guilty asking me something like that. Why guilt? That is a larger question having to do with her upbringing and the expectations that she places on herself and that have been placed on her in the past. So, while she may really want to ask me to take care of dinner so that she can rest, the deeper beliefs of her heart will not allow her to do so.

The same can happen for me. Seemingly trivial questions like, "Are you almost done with the dishes?" can trigger a defensive reaction from me. Why? Because what I'm hearing is a criticism: "Why aren't you doing this fast enough?" In reality, she just might be asking because she needs something from the cabinet above me and does not want to bother me until I'm finished. Again, my reaction is informed by a deeper premise that has little to do with the question my wife was asking me. This too is informed by past experiences.

Through the process of growing in EQ, we have learned to be more self-aware. We have become much more conscious of those underlying beliefs that hinder our communication and have made strides in overcoming those voices from the past that have us reacting negatively in the present. I will not say that we have arrived; in fact, I feel like we are just starting out on this path! But the awareness alone has been invaluable, and the strides we are making are well worth the attention we are giving to it.

If EQ allows us to understand our own purposes better and allows us to understand the purposes of those around us better, can you imagine what this can mean for your relationship with God?

Chapter Three

What Is Emotional Intelligence?

Part I – God's Will and Definitions

Emotions make excellent servants, but tyrannical masters.
—John Seymour

Dear friend, I know that you are spiritually well.
I pray that you're doing well in
every other way and that you're healthy.
—3 John 1:2 (GW)

Based on our culture and family of origin, our view of emotions may be a positive one, a negative one, or a mix of both, depending on which emotion is being considered. Anger is the first emotion that comes to mind that many people have fears about. Ironically, some people even have fears about positive emotions such as joy because they are consciously or unconsciously expecting the "other shoe to drop" if they experience joy. But God created us and our emotions. Just as many of us (especially as we age) are not fired up about how our body is functioning (after the Fall [Genesis 3]), many of us are also disillusioned about the impact of others' emotions on us and the impact of our own emotions on ourselves and our relationships.

Yet, no matter how we feel (no matter what emotions we have) about emotions, we are God's workmanship. He created us to be feeling creatures. We are fearfully and wonderfully made (Psalm 139:13–16). We are God's image bearers (Genesis 1:26) and God's temple (1 Corinthians 6:19). God is not a robot, devoid of emotion. He has deep emotions. He did not make us robots either. Our emotions are an integral part of our humanity and are meant to serve a useful purpose. If we are not happy about that, then we need to better understand God's grace and emotional intelligence. What

God has made is very good (Genesis 1:31)!

In Psalm 51:12-13, David said, "Restore to me the joy of your salvation and grant me a willing spirit, to sustain me. Then I will teach transgressors your ways, so that sinners will turn back to you." This passage gives an example of the impact of our emotions. David makes a conditional statement. He says that when we have the joy of salvation and a willing spirit, we will teach transgressors God's ways so that sinners can be saved. For those who love linear thinking, the emotional hypothesis and behavioral conclusion are clear in this psalm. Science tells us that our emotional state impacts and is interdependent with our physiology and our internal representations. Internal or mental representations are created when we represent the outside world to ourselves. They are our cognitions or the content of our thinking. They are how we represent, in our minds, information entering our brain through our senses. Simply put, **internal representations are how we perceive things in our minds.**

Our internal representations can include pictures, sounds, feelings, tastes, smells, and self-talk. We differ in our internal representations, as two people can experience the same event and have different mental representations or images of it in their minds. For example, one person can have a pleasant internal representation of the vegetable known as okra in their mind. They visualize and possibly even smell a lightly cooked and slightly crisp green and tasty pleasure. Others may have a completely different internal representation of okra: that it is slimy, limp, runny, and completely distasteful. Their internal representation possibly includes a picture of this vegetable, disgusting feelings, an unpleasant taste and smell, and the self-talk that they will avoid it at all costs. Our internal representations are our perceptions. Science and Psalm 51 are aligned here in that our perceptions impact our physiology and emotional state. I have included additional information on science, the brain, and our internal representations in the next chapter, "Master Your Mind."

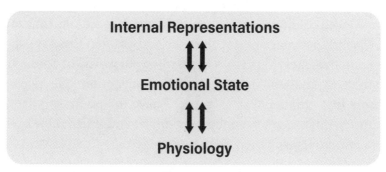

Figure 3:1

"Emotions add pleasure, comfort, and richness to events and relationships" (Mahaney, 2017). They give meaning and depth to our lives. All we have to do to understand that statement better is to imagine ourselves without the emotional reactions to someone getting baptized, losing a parent, having a baby, getting married, getting fired, opening a business, or hurting someone. As you considered that emotionless possibility, you probably were aware of the emotions you have felt in the past with each incident. Our emotions let us know that we are God's human creation, not just another animal on the planet. We are God's beloved children. In Ephesians 4:15 (ESV), God calls us to grow up in every way in Christ. Additional Bible versions note that we are called to grow in every way more and more like Christ (NLT), in all things (KJV, YLT), in all aspects (NASB), completely (ISV), in all our affairs (ABPE), and in every respect (NIV). This includes our ability and skills regarding loving God, ourselves, and others, along with manifesting the fruit of the Holy Spirit. This is emotional intelligence, in a nutshell, from a biblical point of view. Jesus is our ultimate model of EQ!

Most of our ways of handling situations, emotions, and other people have been sculpted since our childhood. It takes the self-awareness of EQ and the practice of building helpful skills to resist repeating unhealthy practices that we learned as children from the significant adults in our lives. We are actually "primed for certain emotional habits" (Goleman, 1995, p. 145), but we have God's word and God's Spirit as the standard and the power to change anything that needs to be brought into better alignment with God's amazing plan for our lives (John 10:10).

God's Will for Our Welfare, Future, and Hope

Efforts to increase your EQ skills may seem a bit daunting, especially if you felt discouraged about your EQ Appraisal® results. But God has a plan for His beloved children. God has a plan for you! Please take time to review and frequently set your mind (Colossians 3:2) on what God says about His plan for our lives and His promises regarding our welfare, hope, and future (Lehner, 2016). These biblical promises and convictions will help us as we dive more into emotional intelligence. I have intentionally included the scriptures in this section from the less familiar Amplified Bible so that our conscious minds can possibly be more engaged.

Our Welfare:

Matthew 6:31–33

"Therefore do not worry or be anxious (perpetually uneasy, distracted), saying, 'What are we going to eat?' or 'What are we going to drink?' or 'What are we going to wear?' For the [pagan] Gentiles eagerly seek all these things; [but do not worry,] for your heavenly Father knows that you need them. But first and most importantly seek (aim at, strive after) His kingdom and His righteousness [His way of doing and being right—the attitude and character of God], and all these things will be given to you also."

1 Corinthians 10:13

No temptation [regardless of its source] has overtaken or enticed you that is not common to human experience [nor is any temptation unusual or beyond human resistance]; but God is faithful [to His word—He is compassionate and trustworthy], and He will not let you be tempted beyond your ability [to resist], but along with the temptation He [has in the past and is now and] will [always] provide the way out as well, so that you will be able to endure it [without yielding, and will overcome temptation with joy].

John 15:11

"I have told you these things so that My joy and delight may be in you, and that your joy may be made full and complete and overflowing."

Hebrews 13:20–21

Now may the God of peace [the source of serenity and spiritual well-being] who brought up from the dead our Lord Jesus, the great Shepherd of the sheep, through the blood that sealed and ratified the eternal covenant, equip you with every good thing to carry out His will and strengthen you [making you complete and perfect as you ought to be], accomplishing in us that which is pleasing in His sight, through Jesus Christ, to whom be the glory forever and ever. Amen.

Ephesians 3:14–16

For this reason [grasping the greatness of this plan by which Jews and Gentiles are joined together in Christ] I bow my KNEES [in reverence] before the Father [of our Lord Jesus Christ], from whom every family in heaven and on earth derives its name [God—the first and ultimate Father]. May He grant you out of the riches of His glory, to be strengthened and spiritually energized with power through His Spirit in your inner self, [indwelling your innermost being and personality].

Hebrews 13:6

So we take comfort and are encouraged and confidently say, "THE LORD IS MY HELPER [in time of need], I WILL NOT BE AFRAID. WHAT WILL MAN DO TO ME?"

Mark 10:29–30

Jesus said, "I assure you and most solemnly say to you, there is no one who has given up a house or brothers or sisters or mother or father or children or farms, for My sake and for the gospel's sake, who will not receive a hundred times as much now in the present age—houses and brothers and sisters and mothers and children and farms—along with persecutions; and in the age to come, eternal life."

John 14:1–3

"Do not let your heart be troubled (afraid, cowardly). Believe [confidently] in God and trust in Him, [have faith, hold on to it, rely on it, keep going and] believe also in Me. In My Father's house are many dwelling places. If it were not so, I would have told you, because I am going there to prepare a place for you. And if I go and prepare a place for you, I will come back again and I will take you to Myself, so that where I am you may be also."

Reflection:

From the above scriptures, what do you understand is God's plan for our welfare? For the states and emotions in the above scriptures (such as worry, joy, temptation, strength, and spirituality) what do you imagine is God's plan for your welfare?

_____

_____

_____

_____

_____

_____

Our Future:

Philippians 1:6

"I am convinced and confident of this very thing, that He who has begun a good work in you will [continue to] perfect and complete it until the day of Christ Jesus [the time of His return].

1 John 3:2

Beloved, we are [even here and] now children of God, and it is not yet made clear what we will be [after His coming]. We know that when He comes and is revealed, we will [as His children] be like Him, because we will see Him just as He is [in all His glory].

Revelation 22:3-5

There will no longer exist anything that is cursed [because sin and illness and death are gone]; and the throne of God and of the Lamb will be in it, and His bond-servants will serve and worship Him [with great awe and joy and loving devotion]; they will [be privileged to] see His face, and His name will be on their foreheads. And there will no longer be night; they have no need for lamplight or sunlight, because the Lord God will illumine them; and they will reign [as kings] forever and ever.

Revelation 21:4

"He will wipe away every tear from their eyes; and there will no longer be death; there will no longer be sorrow and anguish, or crying, or pain; for the former order of things has passed away."

Ephesians 1:16-18

I do not cease to give thanks for you, remembering you in my prayers; [I always pray] that the God of our Lord Jesus Christ, the Father of glory, may grant you a spirit of wisdom and of revelation [that gives you a deep and personal and intimate insight] into the true knowledge of Him [for we know the Father through the Son]. And [I pray] that the eyes of your heart [the very center and core of your being] may be enlightened [flooded with light by the Holy Spirit], so that you will know and cherish the hope [the divine guarantee, the confident expectation] to which He has called you, the riches of His glorious inheritance in the saints (God's people).

Reflection:

From the above scriptures, what do you understand is God's plan for our future?

_____

_____

_____

Our Hope:

Colossians 1:3–5

We give thanks to God, the Father of our Lord Jesus Christ, as we pray always for you, for we have heard of your faith in Christ Jesus [how you lean on Him with absolute confidence in His power, wisdom, and goodness], and of the [unselfish] love which you have for all the saints (God's people); because of the [confident] hope [of experiencing that] which is reserved and waiting for you in heaven. You previously heard of this hope in the message of truth, the gospel [regarding salvation].

1 Thessalonians 4:13

Now we do not want you to be uninformed, believers, about those who are asleep [in death], so that you will not grieve [for them] as the others do who have no hope [beyond this present life].

1 Thessalonians 5:8–10

But since we [believers] belong to the day, let us be sober, having put on the breastplate of faith and love, and as a helmet, the hope and confident assurance of salvation. For God has not destined us to [incur His] wrath [that is, He did not select us to condemn us], but to obtain salvation through our Lord Jesus Christ, who died [willingly] for us, so that whether we are awake (alive) or asleep (dead) [at Christ's appearing], we will live together with Him [sharing eternal life].

1 Peter 1:3–4

Blessed [gratefully praised and adored] be the God and Father of our Lord Jesus Christ, who according to His abundant and boundless mercy has caused us to be born again [that is, to be reborn from above— spiritually transformed, renewed, and set apart for His purpose] to an ever-living hope and confident assurance through the resurrection of Jesus Christ from the dead, [born anew] into an inheritance which is imperishable [beyond the reach of change] and undefiled and unfading, reserved in heaven for you.

1 Peter 1:21

Through Him you believe [confidently] in God [the heavenly Father], who raised Him from the dead and gave Him glory, so that your faith and hope are [centered and rest] in God.

2 Peter 1:3

For His divine power has bestowed on us [absolutely] everything necessary for [a dynamic spiritual] life and godliness.

Reflection:

From the scriptures above, what do you see as God's plan for our hope?

_____

_____

_____

How do these scriptures make you feel?

_____

_____

_____

Are your thoughts (internal representations) about the scriptures on your personal welfare, future, and hope generally positive or negative?

_____

_____

_____

Has your behavior been positively impacted by the scriptures on your personal welfare, future, and hope?

_____

_____

_____

Please keep the aforementioned scriptures in mind as we do a deeper dive into EQ. Only with a healthy level of emotional intelligence along with healthy neural circuits and internal representations will our emotions, thoughts, and relationships be impacted and transformed by God's word as He intended (Romans 12:2). For too much of my life, I was stuck with both the harmful emotional residue of emotions like anger, sadness, fear, hurt, and guilt, and with limiting beliefs and decisions that did not leave room for God's word to permeate my heart, mind, soul, and strength. Many times, I felt that I did not have strength, that I was doomed to negativity and depression, and that the constant efforts to set my mind just did not work—they did not reach my emotions/heart. With EQ and the advances in neuroscience and therapeutic techniques, we can better internalize God's word and His plan for our EQ, lives, welfare, future, and hope!

Definitions

Before we discuss in further detail God's view on emotional intelligence, we must know and understand what emotions and EQ are. It is essential that we define the words we will discuss. You have likely had the experience of conversing with someone about a topic and at some point, after it seems like you are two ships passing in the night, you realize that you don't perceive the main topics and words the same as the other person in the conversation. This can happen not only with spiritual topics, but in every area of our lives. Thus, clarifying definitions is critical.

Emotions

Historical background about EQ will be helpful. In 1990, Peter Salovey and John Mayer coined the term "emotional intelligence." In 1995, Daniel Goleman published his first book on the topic, titled *Emotional Intelligence.* Regarding the book *Emotional Intelligence 2.0* (2009), the Dalai Lama notes that Bradberry and Greaves' book "succinctly explains how to deal with emotions creatively and employ our intelligence in a beneficial way." In the TalentSmart® Discovering or Mastering Emotional Intelligence workshop (2016), emotions are defined as: "a physiological experience which manifests itself in neuro-muscular, respiratory, cardiovascular, and hormonal changes including modifications in thought and behavior." "Emotions are complex and have both physical and mental components. Researchers agree that emotions have the following parts: subjective feelings, physiological (body) responses, and expressive behavior" (*Human Diseases,* n.d.).

When we have seen people out of control with anger or if we don't have a handle on our own emotions, we may wonder why we have emotions and have to deal with them at all. God created us as emotional beings. Our emotions are one of the traits that make us humans. From our emotions we have creativity, the arts, the ability to effectively relate to others, and even an opportunity for survival (flight or fight response). Daniel Goleman (1995) shares that emotions are evolution-instilled impulses to act. The root of the word "emotion," is the Latin verb *motere,* which means to move, and the prefix "e" means away. The meaning implies that with each emotion comes a tendency to act (Goleman). "Just as our minds enable us to think and our wills enable us to choose, so our emotions enable us to respond" (Mahaney, 2017).

When I looked up the word "emotions" in a thesaurus, I saw a list of different emotions. But when I looked up the word "feelings" I found synonyms such as emotions, desires, passions, affection, impressions, concerns, and sensations. Wake Forest University (n.d.) informs us that, "A fundamental difference between feelings and emotions is that feelings are experienced consciously, while emotions manifest either consciously or subconsciously. Some people may spend years, or even a lifetime, not understanding the depths of their emotions." Emotions tell us about what we value, believe, and desire. Emotions also point to inclinations that affect our behavior. Donna Hart (2016) notes that "emotions are the language of the soul; they are the cries that give the heart a voice. God gave them to us to energize our behavior and to be a catalyst for action." God does not want us to be robots or to be our taskmaster. He wants our hearts. He has even commanded us to love Him with all our heart, soul, mind, and strength (Mark 12:29–30). What we feel and what is going on in our hearts is of great importance to God. The Bible says that this command is the first and greatest commandment (v. 31). Our thoughts and emotions drive our behavior and thus play a major role in our lives. It would be prideful (an overused term at times) to inadequately address our hearts and souls since God has clearly spoken about their importance.

Emotional Intelligence

In the Mastering Emotional Intelligence™ workshop, Greaves (2016) defines Emotional Intelligence as: "your ability to recognize and understand emotions, and your *skill* at using this awareness to manage yourself and your relationships with others." Workshop participants frequently laugh when I inform them that it will be easy to remember the word RUM. It is a great acrostic for understanding and remembering a description of emotional intelligence. One who is emotionally intelligent can (RUM):

Recognize emotions, **U**nderstand emotions, and **M**anage emotions.

In addition, the four parts, or core skills, of emotional intelligence are based on a connection between what we see and what we do with ourselves and others (Emotional Intelligence Appraisal®, 2016). The four core EQ skills (Figure 3.2) include self-awareness, self-management, social awareness, and relationship management. An informal evaluation of self-awareness asks, "Can I accurately identify my own emotions and tendencies as they happen?" Self-management asks, "Can I manage my emotions and behavior to a positive outcome?" An assessment of social awareness asks, "Can I accurately identify others' emotions and tendencies as I interact with them or a group?" With both self- and social awareness, we need to consider the entire picture of what's going on. This includes what's going on beneath the surface. The Emotion Iceberg (see "Our Conscious and Unconscious Minds" in Chapter 4, Part II) has typically been used to explain that much of what is going on is deep waters (Proverbs 20:5). Lastly, relationship management asks, "Can I manage the interactions I have with others constructively and to a positive outcome?" With relationship management we also consider if both individual needs and task requirements are met in our interactions. "Emotional intelligence is a master aptitude, a capacity that profoundly affects all other abilities, either facilitating or interfering with them" (Goleman, 1995, p. 80). The figure below summarizes EQ skills.

Four Core EQ Skills	
What We See	**What We Do**
Self-Awareness Can I accurately identify my own emotions and tendencies as they happen?	**Self-Management** Can I manage my emotions and behavior to a positive outcome?
Social Awareness Can I accurately identify others' emotions and tendencies as I interact with them or a group?	**Relationship Management** Can I manage the interactions I have with others constructively and to a positive outcome?

Reflection:
Which definition resonates most? Answer the four questions in Figure 3.2.

_____

_____

_____

_____

_____

_____

Where Does EQ Come From?

Most of us have likely not given much thought to how our unconscious mind operates. It is now fairly common knowledge that our unconscious/subconscious mind controls most of our thinking. Ninety-five percent of our behaviors come from our subconscious. Scientists and researchers report that this part of God's creation, our subconscious, is largely formed before we reach the age of six or seven. Our brains really are like a tape recorder where neural circuits/networks are laid down every day of our lives. I'm sure you have heard of parents reading or speaking to a child in utero (during pregnancy), or have done this yourself. It is believed that babies can sense love, stress, language, soothing, anxiety, and trauma before birth. Parenting impacts the brain development of children.

> For the growing brain of a young child, the social world supplies the most important experiences influencing the expression of genes, which determines how neurons connect to one another in creating the neuronal pathways which give rise to mental activity. (Lipton, 2016)

As children develop, they pick up skills and learn through observation. Learning or not learning EQ skills happens the same way. We really are sponges during the early years.

Neurologically, as events are repeated in a child's life, the child subconsciously records the emotional messages and lessons that can determine their life course. We first learn about emotions from our family life. We learn how to feel about ourselves, how others react to our feelings, how to think about feelings, and even the choices we have in reacting to our feelings and emotions. We learn how to read others' emotions and how to express emotions. These lessons not only come from what significant adults "say and do directly to children, but also in the models they offer for handling their own feelings and those that pass between husband and wife" (Goleman, 1995, p. 190). Goleman notes that "some parents are gifted emotional teachers, others atrocious" (p. 190). Parents' behavior and beliefs become the child's own (Lipton, 2016).

Research has shown that couples who are emotionally competent are most effective in managing their children's emotions. Goleman (1995) reports that ignoring feelings altogether, being too laissez-faire, and being contemptuous of a child's feelings were the most common emotionally inept parenting styles. For children to have emotional intelligence skills, their parents need to model self-awareness, self-management, social awareness, and relationship management skills. An encouraging facet of EQ is that with healthy EQ skills, children fare better physically/biologically, socially, emotionally, and academically (Goleman). Children's confidence, curiosity, boundaries, school readiness, ability to learn, academic achievement and school success, impulsiveness or self-control, relatedness, communication ability, and cooperativeness are all based on the emotional intelligence foundation provided by their caregivers. Children need not only a Head Start, but also a "Heart Start" (Goleman). Our hearts matter to God. Our spiritual maturity is dependent upon our EQ skills, which are foundational for success in every area of our lives. Fortunately, we can develop and strengthen our EQ skills.

Chapter Three—Part I Summary

This chapter included a large amount of information. Great job combing through it! In order to internalize what you have read and reflected upon, please select the three main points that resonated with you.

To anchor your **top three learnings** or (new or deepened) convictions, list them here:

_____

_____

_____

You can thoroughly anchor your learnings by making at least **one decision** on how to implement what you have learned. If your decision can be written in the SMART (Specific, Measurable, Attainable/Achievable, Relevant, and Timed) format, you will have a better chance of it becoming a reality! Record your **one SMART decision** here:

_____

_____

_____

_____

_____

_____

Part II – The Four Skills of Emotional Intelligence

In Part II of this chapter we will discuss the definitions and concepts of self-awareness, self-management, social awareness, and relationship management. How we can apply EQ science to our spiritual transformation efforts is also discussed.

Self-awareness

Self-awareness is being aware of our emotions or moods and our thoughts about those emotions. Self-awareness is especially important since we cannot have self-control (self-discipline [2 Timothy 1:7]) without being aware of what needs to be managed. In 1 Timothy 4:16, God in His infinite wisdom tells us, "Keep a close watch on yourself and on the teaching. Persist in this, for by so doing you will save both yourself and your hearers" (ESV). Life without self-awareness will result in all types of headaches and dysfunctions. Life with self-awareness has been found to lead to clarity, autonomy, healthy boundaries, good psychological health, and a positive outlook on life (Goleman, 1995).

You have likely heard the term "mindfulness." This conscious self-awareness can help us get out of bad moods more quickly. Even more interesting, Goleman (1995) describes two ends of a self-awareness spectrum, where we either feel overwhelmed by the awareness of our emotions or are not aware of the emotions at all. You may not be surprised that women, in general, feel emotions more strongly than do men (Goleman). More importantly, "sex differences aside, emotional life is richer for those who notice more" (Goleman, p. 50). Psychotherapy typically attempts to increase self-awareness and psychological insight, since EQ is built on self-awareness.

Goleman's (1995) compilation of research shows that about 17% of people tune out emotions. Instead of calling them repressors, Goleman called these people "unflappables." Fascinatingly, in one study, repressor research participants were not consciously aware of their emotions, but the emotions were evident in their physiology. In study after study, our self-awareness and emotional aptitude (or our EQ) has been shown to affect every area of our lives—academic achievement, workplace success, relationships, communication, teamwork, decision-making, critical thinking, time management, stress tolerance, flexibility, trust, and more.

We can work on being more aware of our emotions as well as expressing our emotions more appropriately. Culturally, the display of emotions varies. Yet, since we are designed by God with emotions, managing them in a godly way benefits us all. We can either ignore, minimize, magnify, dramatize, or substitute emotions. As we have seen, very often, our self-awareness is learned through the models we have in early life. Our display of emotions immediately impacts our internal representations, physiology (Figure 3.1), and those around us. Emotions are also contagious (Goleman, 1995). You may have seen the viral videos where laughter and even smiling is contagious. We can either share toxicity or nourishment. We can take captive every thought (2 Corinthians 10:5) so that the impact on ourselves and others is one of positivity.

During one of my early counseling sessions, my therapist introduced Eye Movement Desensitization and Reprocessing (EMDR) to attempt to relieve the psychological stress of a traumatic event. With the EMDR process, she shared a list of negative and positive cognitions (listed under resources on www.cresendajones.com). She asked me to read the left column of cognitions or beliefs. The negative list was very easy for me to read. Statements such as "I do not deserve love," "I am worthless," "I should have known better," and "I am powerless" were listed under negative cognitions. They felt familiar and true. The positive list of cognitions, located on the right side, elicited a deep sadness. As I read the first cognition, "I deserve love; I can have love," I ended up sobbing for a while. I realized that I did not believe that I deserved love nor did I believe that I could have it. Neither parent ever said, "I don't love you" or "You don't deserve to be loved," but, since they both were emotionally unavailable and often seemed to be self-absorbed, that is the message I received/perceived.

It is amazing how closely entwined our thoughts (internal representations or cognitions) and our emotions are. Of course, negative thoughts/beliefs, even subconscious ones, negatively impact our emotional state (as displayed in Figure 3.1). During those sessions in the early 2000s, my therapist noted that she thought I had been depressed for around 20 years. Goleman notes that "we catch feelings from one another as though they were some kind of social virus" (1995, p. 115). Even if we are not aware of the emotions, we send emotional signals with every interaction.

How does this magical transmission occur? The most likely answer is that we unconsciously imitate the emotions we see displayed by someone else, through an out-of-awareness motor mimicry of their facial expression, gestures, tone of voice, and other nonverbal markers of emotion. (Goleman, 1995, p. 115)

Though I was not aware of my state of depression, I seemed to unconsciously imitate the emotions I experienced at home.

I'm immensely grateful that our emotions "are a part of our humanity that needs to be sanctified and brought under the authority of God's word. The redemptive process is intended for the whole person; and emotions are an inherent component of our personhood" (Hart, 2016). **We cannot heal that with which we are unwilling to deal.** It is foolish and unwise to ignore our heart, soul, emotions, and feelings. We cannot rectify and bring under the authority of God things that we are not aware of. Spiritual transformation and emotional intelligence are built on the foundation of self-awareness.

As with many good habits and skills, self-reflection is most valuable when done consistently. Here are a few questions you can periodically ask yourself and even discuss with others to strengthen your self-awareness muscles and skills:

1. When am I at my best?
2. What kind of person do I want to be today?
3. What situations make me feel terrible, and what do they have in common?
4. What activities am I doing when it feels like time flies by?
5. What is working well in my life and work today?
6. If I had a magic wand, how would my life be better in three months?
7. If I change nothing, what will my life look like three months from now? A year from now? Ten years from now? How does this make me feel?
8. What actions, if taken, would make me proud of myself, regardless of the outcome?
9. When negative thoughts arise, how do I deal with them?
10. How do I stay grounded when I feel overwhelmed?
11. What motivates me to make progress?
12. Am I living as a person of integrity? (Wilding, 2019)

"The goal isn't to answer immediately or to have a perfectly formulated response to each inquiry. The deepest work is in the art of asking, and attuning to what arises, so it can lead you back to yourself" (Wilding, 2019). "The purposes of a person's heart are deep waters, but one who has insight draws them out" (Proverbs 20:5). As you work to increase self-awareness, if at any time your emotions and thoughts become overwhelming, reach out to a trusted and safe friend or professional. *Emotional Intelligence 2.0* lists and describes 15 strategies for increasing self-awareness (p. 63). In Chapter 8, I have included a resource list of scriptures for the 15 strategies.

Reflection:

Can I accurately identify my own emotions and tendencies as they happen? Reviewing your Emotional Intelligence Appraisal® *results can provide objective insight.*

_____

_____

_____

What are your values? What is most important to you about life, relationships, and success? Write a list (empty out all thoughts) and then come back to the list at least twice to add anything else that is important to you (empty out each time). Then number the list in order of importance and record your top six values in order.

_____

_____

_____

_____

_____

_____

Do I understand why I do the things I do? Am I aware of my motives and the emotions, beliefs, and values that drive my behavior?

_____

_____

_____

Have I classified any feelings and emotions as either good or bad (either vilified or prohibited)—anger, sadness, fear, hurt, guilt, joy, gratitude, hope, serenity, confidence, love, etc.? Are my convictions about emotions based on the Bible or on those who were the significant adults (models) in my childhood?

_____

_____

_____

How much do I know myself under stress? Do I heed the warning signs of stress and recharge my emotional batteries?

_____

_____

_____

Regarding the second reflection question (values), where is God or spirituality on your list? To what extent is there room for God to be of greater value? What type of life does the Bible say results from how we value God? (Isaiah 40:31; Deuteronomy 30:19 CEV).

_____

_____

_____

Self-Management

You may have heard some variation of the saying, feelings/emotions make wonderful servants but horrible masters! The Romans and the early Christian church called self-management *temperantia* or temperance, the restraining of emotional excess (Goleman, 1995, p. 56). Goleman furthermore describes self-mastery as being able to withstand the emotional storms that life brings us. In *Emotional Intelligence*, Goleman also defines self-control as "the ability to modulate and control one's own actions in age-appropriate ways; a sense of inner control" (p. 194).

For many, extremely intense emotions are experienced only periodically, yet we all experience a steady stream, or hum, of thoughts and emotions that we need to process. From the time we are infants, either we learn to soothe ourselves well, or we don't. I starkly remember a dear sister who felt that she just could and would not conquer her sexual urges.

After reading her recovery workbook, with permission, I saw where she was able to articulate that at a very young age, she started self-soothing sexually in response to her fear after hearing her parents' frequent verbal and physical fights at night when they thought she was asleep. She didn't know how to handle the fear, fright, and trauma, but she figured out a way to soothe herself and quiet her emotions. Unfortunately, after years of such activity, she led a life of promiscuity and adultery, which subsequently led to her being asked to no longer be a part of a church fellowship. (Please review Matthew 18:17, 1 Corinthians 5:9–11, and 2 Thessalonians 3:14 for more clarity on this.) Her situation broke my heart, and I became more determined than ever to provide additional tools and practical answers for HOW we can be more emotionally intelligent and spiritually mature. Without healthy self-soothing and self-control skills, it becomes easier to reach cognitive incapacitation where we are totally controlled by our emotions and we "lose it." According to John Bowlby and D. W. Winnicott, self-soothing is "one of the most essential of all psychic tools" (Goleman, 1995, p. 57).

In regard to self-management, researchers have found that "children who can't read or express emotions well constantly feel frustrated" (Goleman, 1995, p. 122). Imagine how socially frustrated, isolated, rejected, and neglected one would be after years of compounding EQ deficits. We also learn through biblical self-awareness that **positive emotional states generally are a choice.** We cannot always control how we are feeling, but we can control our reactions to our emotions. If we react to negative stimuli in a healthy manner, it may help us to clear away some of our more destructive thoughts and feelings (Kunst, 2016).

We all can choose to increase our emotional self-management skills and avoid the harmful attempts of escape through addiction to food, shopping, sex, sports, drugs, alcohol, TV, pornography, achievement, work, service, social media, religion, busyness, or something else. Healthy soothing leaves us "less vulnerable to the upheavals of the emotional brain" (Goleman, p. 57).

> As we have seen, the design of the brain means that we very often have little or no control over when we are swept by emotion, nor over what emotion it will be. But we can have some say in how long an emotion will last. (Goleman, p. 57)

On their own, triggered emotions can only last 60–90 seconds (Myles, 2015), which is to say that if the feelings last longer than that, we are now the ones feeding the emotions. On the other hand, ignoring emotions leads to dullness, disconnection, and distance. If we allow our emotions to be out of control, too extreme, or too persistent, they can become pathological (Goleman, 1995). With God, His Spirit, and efforts to build EQ skills, we can strike healthy balances. Even today, I had to play a meditation audio a couple of times and listen to my Time Line Therapy® learnings to sooth some fear and anxiety. Amen for effective tools!

EMDR was somewhat helpful for processing my grief, but I was still left with the toxic emotional residue that was connected to the trauma I experienced in seventh grade. I have been thrilled to learn about Time Line Therapy®, which is used to eliminate harmful emotional residue and limiting beliefs/decisions connected to past events. The Time Line Therapy® transformation process allows us to experience appropriate and warranted levels of emotions as opposed to out-of-proportion feelings due to past emotional baggage. Joe Dispenza has noted that a memory without the emotional charge is called wisdom. And in James 1:5, God promises to generously provide the wisdom we need. I will share more about this amazing process in Chapter 9. We can live lives of healthy emotional self-regulation in which we are not slaves (Romans 6:18) to emotions and emotional hijackings. As the *Names of God Bible* notes, "We are no longer slaves to sin. The person who has died [in baptism] has been freed from sin.... So consider yourselves dead to sin's power but living for God in the power Christ **Yeshua** gives you" (Romans 6:6b–7, 11).

Furthermore, we can reject being paralyzed by our emotions. With awareness of ourselves and our emotions, we can develop greater skills to successfully manage our emotions to our desired outcomes. We are not at the mercy of our moods! "In all these things we are more than conquerors through him who loved us" (Romans 8:37). Our goal is to imitate Jesus, as He was the absolute model of self-control. His emotions (and actions) were warranted and appropriate at all times. I am incredibly grateful for the tools God has provided that help us in this lifelong journey!

With regard to self-management, Goleman (1995) states that

> There is perhaps no psychological skill more fundamental than resisting impulse. It is the root of all emotional self-control, since all emotions, by their very nature, lead to one or another impulse to act.

The root meaning of the word "emotion," remember, is "to move." (p. 81)

Indeed, "'goal-directed self-imposed delay of gratification' is perhaps the essence of emotional self-regulation: the ability to deny impulse in the service of a goal" (Goleman, 1995, p. 83). "Emotions out of control impede the intellect" (Goleman, 1995, p. 86). With God, His Spirit, and rewiring our subconscious neural circuits (using Time Line Therapy®), we can live as emotionally intelligent disciples of Christ.

Reflection:

Which life goals, beliefs, and values do you choose to guide your impulse control?

_____

_____

_____

To what extent do you possess emotional integrity? Are you able to consistently act in accordance with your deepest values no matter the results or consequences?

_____

_____

_____

Daniel Goleman (1995) notes that "channeling emotions toward a productive end is a master aptitude" (p. 95). Can you consistently manage your emotions and behavior to a positive outcome?

_____

_____

_____

Our toxic and inappropriate emotional residue can lead to self-fulfilling prophecies because of how our brains operate. Thus, it is imperative that we build self-management skills so that we can harness our emotions and direct them toward our desired outcomes. Remember that God is totally for us. Since He created our brains and knows how they work, even after the Fall, He instructs us to rejoice always, pray without ceasing, and give thanks (1 Thessalonians 5:16–18). This is God's will for us in Christ Jesus. God is the originator of the "power of positive thinking"!

Even Goleman (1995) found that hope makes all the difference as we approach challenges. As disciples **we can choose** to continually have hope in God. As Psalm 46:1–3 notes,

> God is our refuge and strength,
>   an ever-present help in trouble.
> Therefore **we will not fear,** though the earth give way
>   and the mountains fall into the heart of the sea,
> though its waters roar and foam
>   and the mountains quake with their surging. (emphasis added)

Take a few moments to think about that—visualize this scripture. Meditate and reflect on what the psalmist is stating. Imagine that the earth gives way and the mountains fall into the sea. What would your response be? Would you choose fear or peace? Would you feel connected to God's ever-present help? Trusting God does not mean that our lives will always be carefree and without challenge. Sometimes our world will fall apart. Sometimes the mountains will "fall into the heart of the sea." Yet, with self-management, we can direct our minds and emotions to the state exhibited in the song *It Is Well With my Soul*. It is awesome to know that we have this choice! In our quest to be like Jesus and to be spiritually mature, emotional regulation is imperative. *Emotional Intelligence 2.0* lists and describes 17 strategies for increasing self-management or self-control (p. 100). In Chapter 8, I have included a resource list of scriptures for the 17 strategies.

Social Awareness

Social awareness asks the question, Can I accurately identify others' emotions and tendencies as I interact with them or a group? (Figure 3.2). It is the ability to accurately pick up on the thoughts, feelings, and emotions of others and understand what is really going on with them (Bradberry & Greaves, 2009). Social awareness includes being aware of unspoken social cues and the mood in the room. One with social awareness understands the culture of organizations and others even if they do not feel the same way.

This EQ skill is built upon self-awareness and self-management, which are both required for healthy social awareness. Without the ability to regulate one's own emotions, it is less likely that one will have the capacity to be attuned to the emotions of others. Empathy, listening, and observing are some of the most important elements of social awareness. Capacity for these social awareness elements depends on our own emotional health. Further, those with healthy social awareness skills can even mirror someone else's emotions and help them to feel a "sense of being deeply acknowledged and understood" (Goleman, 1995, p. 102). This is how we build rapport.

Goleman (1995, p. 96) notes that "empathy builds on self-awareness; the more open we are to our own emotions, the more skilled we will be in reading feelings." A lack of emotional perception is harmful to our personal life and to the relationships we need to have in order to live life as God has planned in His kingdom (1 Corinthians 12:12–27). The ability to build rapport is required for healthy relationships. Social awareness or emotional attunement allows us to develop rapport, the root of caring (Goleman, 1995). Those with social competence can accurately "notice, interpret, and respond to emotional and interpersonal cues" (Goleman, 1995, p. 123).

I feel sad when friends share that they believe/feel that someone ignored them on purpose or that they are not getting their needs met. In such situations, I am made all the more aware of the idea that we cannot love as Jesus did if we don't have the capacity for social awareness. Even if we typically "live in our own world," consumed with our own emotions, problems, and lives, developing EQ skills will increase our capacity to support and love each other. Our greatest commands are centered around loving God and loving others. Living "at capacity" or feeling overwhelmed emotionally will deter us from God's will for our lives. Jesus was able to see that others had needs, and He was able to address those needs. "When he saw the crowds, he had compassion on them, because they were harassed and helpless, like sheep without a shepherd" (Matthew 9:13).

Empathy seems to have disappeared from many subcultures. The divide between religious groups, "races" (merely a social construct), and political parties does not seem to be improving. "Tribalism" has at times destroyed kindness to others and the love that God commands. Sometimes we can be so focused on ourselves or attaining our goals that we forget the other humans in our midst. Unhealthy emotional detachment or dissociation serves no one. It is not humane. It is not God's will. It is a character defect or a deficit. Our goal is not to be free of emotions, but to manage them well. We can claim that we love others when we understand their hearts and their emotions, as 1 Corinthians 13:4–7 indicates. Empathy is a core component of emotional intelligence. *Emotional Intelligence* 2.0 lists and describes 17 strategies for increasing social awareness (p. 138). In Chapter 8, I have included a resource list of scriptures for the 17 strategies.

Reflection:

Are you able to consistently stop everything and listen fully when another person is speaking? Are you able to consistently "stay in the moment" and be present? Are you able to put the phone down or turn off the computer? Are you able to turn off the TV, listen, focus, and have a conversation while you share meals with others?

_____

_____

_____

How many questions do you typically ask about a situation before giving your opinion? Are you able to draw out the deep waters of a person's heart (Proverbs 20:5) through empathy, listening, and questioning?

_____

_____

_____

When do you find it effortless to step into someone else's shoes? Are you typically able to pick up on how someone is feeling? When is it more challenging for you to step into someone else's shoes?

_____

_____

_____

Are you characteristically emotionally and spiritually healthy enough to put aside your own beliefs, emotions, thinking patterns, and tendencies in order to experience a situation the way someone else would—your spouse, parents, children, close friends, leaders, coworkers, boss, subordinates, etc.? (Keep in mind that empathy does not always equal endorsement.)

_____

_____

_____

Bradberry and Greaves (2009) say "what others say about you is usually more accurate than what you think about yourself" (p. 172). In what ways do you agree?

_____

_____

_____

Relationship Management

God wants us to be connected to each other and to accomplish His will for our lives (1 Corinthians 12:12–27)! TalentSmart® describes relationship management as the ability to "manage relationships by building, strengthening, and deepening your connections with the people in your social network" (2011). It asks, Can I manage the interactions I have with others constructively and to a positive outcome? Interpersonal power requires our previous three core EQ skills of self-awareness, self-management, and social awareness. To effectively manage others' emotions and our relationships with others, we must first be able to understand and manage ourselves. Relationship management has also been termed people skills, social competence, social intelligence, and interpersonal intelligence. Without these skills, interpersonal disasters will likely repeat themselves. "These social abilities allow one to shape an encounter, to mobilize and inspire others, to thrive in intimate relationships, to persuade and influence, to put others at ease" (Goleman, 1995. p. 113).

> *Love is patient, love is kind. It does not envy, it does not boast, it is not proud. It does not dishonor others, it is not self-seeking, it is not easily angered, it keeps no record of wrongs. Love does not delight in evil but rejoices with the truth. It always protects, always trusts, always hopes, always perseveres. Love never fails.* (1 Corinthians 13:4–8)

When I think of models of relationship management, I think of Jesus. No one on earth loved like Jesus did. No one has sacrificed as Jesus has. Jesus modeled the love described in 1 Corinthians 13. He perfectly embodied patience, kindness, humility, contentment, modesty, meekness, honor and respect, self-sacrifice, calmness, forgiveness, and good will. Jesus rejoiced with the truth as opposed to delighting in evil. Jesus always protected, trusted, hoped, and persevered. There has never been a more amazing person!

Reflection:

Consider how you need to be more like Jesus today and this week. Consider relationships at home, at work, in your community, in your extended family, and in your fellowship.

Complete the following 1 Corinthians 13 description of love statements that can transform your relationships this week:

I am patient with: _____

I am kind to: _____

Instead of envy, I am grateful for:

_____

_____

_____

Instead of boasting or dishonoring another, I will encourage and lift up: _____

_____

Instead of displaying ego or insecurity, I will work to see myself the way God does (John 3:16) by:

_____

_____

_____

Instead of being consumed with my own issues, needs, and problems, I will be curious and concerned about what is going on with:

_____

_____

_____

Instead of rushing to anger, I will ask at least seven questions about the situation with:

_____

_____

Instead of bitterness about how I've been treated, I will thank God for His forgiveness for my:

_____

_____

_____

Instead of focusing on all the evil in the world, I will rejoice and meditate on the following truths:

_____

_____

_____

Who can I do a better job protecting, trusting, having hope in, and persevering with this week?

_____

_____

_____

Daniel Goleman (1995) aptly informed us that

> People who are able to help others soothe their feelings have an especially valued social commodity; they are the souls others turn to when in greatest emotional need. We are all part of each other's tool kit for emotional change, for better or for worse. (p. 115)

Our relationship management—our degree of rapport with others, our ability to be vulnerable, and our emotional connection—is fueled by our own self-awareness and social awareness. On the other hand, a lack of self-awareness and social awareness can greatly harm our ability to have healthy relationships. I am reminded of the directives on an airplane when there is an emergency: put your own oxygen mask on first before you help others. We can further build our EQ skills in order to live more like Jesus and lovingly support those around us! If we have our personal emotional oxygen in times of duress, we are then able to help other people.

Furthermore, since work or school takes up around 50% of our waking hours, EQ skills in those environments are as important as EQ skills with our families and friends. Goleman (1995) reports that neither academic talent nor IQ are good predictors of job productivity. Studies have shown that rapport and informal networks more aptly determine work success and productivity (Goleman). Moreover, with our increasingly knowledge-based service and work environments, "teams become the work unit rather than the individual himself. And that suggests why emotional intelligence, the skills that help people harmonize, should become increasingly valued as a workplace asset in the years to come" (Goleman, p. 159–196). EQ, not IQ, has been found to be the single most important element in group intelligence. With EQ, groups can have social harmony and successfully complete the tasks at hand. Additionally, Goleman found that "there is virtually no relationship between being an expert and being seen as someone people can trust with their secrets, doubts, and vulnerabilities" (p. 162). Though we need to be examples in our work productivity and success, we can also be go-to people for those around us.

It is not pleasing to God that we would be baptizers, producers, knowledge brokers, or leaders if we do not display the love of Christ through our social competence. We would likely be considered clanging cymbals (1 Corinthians 13:1)—Bible thumpers or doctrine police. It continues to be interesting to see Christians ignore their emotional maturity levels (self-awareness, self-control, social awareness, and relationship management) and at times overcompensate with "knowledge," striving, technical excellence, people-pleasing, serving, leading, or co-opting the term "introvert." Since I had personally suppressed my emotions for such a long time, I lived this way, even as a disciple. It is especially interesting to see this play out time and time again on social media. Let's continue to encourage each other and speak the truth in love so that God will be glorified by our lives. *Emotional Intelligence 2.0* lists and describes 17 strategies for increasing relationship management (p. 179). In Chapter 8, I have included a resource list of scriptures for the 17 strategies.

In short, "emotional intelligence is a master aptitude, a capacity that profoundly affects all other abilities, either facilitating or interfering with them" (Goleman, 1995, p. 80). With high EQ skill levels, we have healthier moods, clearer and more flexible thinking, better problem solving, and more fulfilling relationships and marriages. We always have choices regarding how we respond to emotions. The more ways we know HOW to respond and the more EQ skills we have, the richer our lives can be!

May the God who gives endurance and encouragement give you the same attitude of mind toward each other that Christ Jesus had, so that with one mind and one voice you may glorify the God and Father of our Lord Jesus Christ. (Romans 15:5-6)

_____ Chapter Three—Part II Summary _____

This chapter included an immense amount of information. Great job combing through it! In order to internalize what you have read and reflected upon, please select the three main points that resonated with you.

To anchor your **top three learnings** or (new or deepened) convictions, list them here:

_____

_____

_____

You can more thoroughly anchor your learnings by making at least **one decision** on how to implement what you have learned. If your decision can be written in the SMART (Specific, Measurable, Attainable/Achievable, Relevant, and Timed) format, you will have a better chance of it becoming a reality! Record your **one SMART decision** here:

_____

_____

_____

Chapter Four

Master Your Mind

Part I – Mind the Basics

The brain is the hardware of the soul.
—HHS (Amen, 2005)

The conscious mind determines the actions, the unconscious
mind determines the reactions;
and the reactions are just as important as the actions.
—E. Stanley Jones

Did you know that:

1. Your brain is involved in everything you do and who you are.

2. When your brain works right, you work right. When your brain doesn't work right, you can't work right.

3. The human brain is the most complex organ in the universe.

4. The brain is very soft, sometimes described to be like a soft-boiled egg or butter.

5. Certain brain systems are involved with certain behaviors.

6. Problems in specific parts of your brain tend to cause specific symptoms.

7. Most psychiatric illnesses are not single or simple disorders.

8. Looking at the brain via imaging scans helps doctors and psychiatrists be more effective.

9. Our brains can change! The right interventions help. Wrong interventions hurt (Amen, 2005).

Our goal is to be what God intends: "mature and complete, not lacking anything" (James 1:4)! In order to optimize the functioning of our brain, we need to know what we have. To effectively manage everything in our world, we need to first have awareness and then work toward greater knowledge and understanding. Though some of us were required to take an anatomy class in high school, most of us have probably not given much thought to how important our brain is. Understanding how our brain or our mind works is not typically included in everyday conversations. God made this astounding organ (Psalm 139:14). Everything He created is important and is to be cared for, thought of and loved. With effective tools, we can all "learn to balance and optimize the parts of the brain responsible for inner growth, intimacy, and spiritual health" (Amen, 2005) to become the people we want to be and whom God wants us to be. With the power of our brain and the all-pervasive impact it has on our lives and spirituality, it is imperative that we understand at least the basics of how it functions.

Reflection:

Which facts about the brain surprised you?

_____

_____

_____

How much thought have you given to how your brain operates and what it needs to operate optimally?

_____

_____

_____

What do you know about your brain and its functioning that helps you optimally manage your everyday life (thoughts, actions, feelings, relationships)?

_____

_____

_____

_____

_____

Please name (list below) something/anything that is not connected to psychology:

_____

_____

_____

If we can *think* about something, it is connected to psychology (APA video, n.d.). Understanding the meaning of important terms is critical. For our general purposes, we can refer to an online dictionary for the definition of psychology. Psychology has been defined as the science of the mind or of mental states and processes and the science of human and animal behavior (www.dictionary.com). Psychology has also been defined as the study of the soul, our deepest self or essence.

Psychology helps us to better understand ourselves and our world. All the things that matter to us in our world are related to psychology: spirituality, love, safety, family dynamics, education, happiness, housing, work relationships, work-life balance, community, motivation, life satisfaction, religion, culture, hunger, sleep, hormones, behavior, drugs, laughter, and smiling. Business, ethics, diversity, relationship skills, cognition, social and cultural issues, how we influence each other, how the brain functions and processes, memory and how one learns, mental health, personalities, human and child development, human sexuality, managing stress, critical and analytical skills, creativity, relationship skills, peer pressure, physical health, and even our environment are all related to psychology.

> In Greek the word for "soul" is *psyche,* from which we get the word psychology. The soul involves the mind and emotions. It gives us the capacity to relate to others and to form bonds. It is our souls that respond to beauty and high ideals. People with healthy souls are capable of forming meaningful relationships, and people with unhealthy souls find it more difficult. Soul care is the attention given to healing a wounded soul or maintaining a healthy soul. In a Christian context, soul care is often linked to finding help to overcome temptations, fight addictions, and have peace with God. (Got Questions Ministries, 2012–2019)

As you know, God calls us to love Him with all our soul and with all our mind in scriptures such as Matthew 22:37, Mark 12:30, and Luke 10:27.

Our Brain, Personality, and Emotions

We have all heard of people "losing it" as we listen to coworkers, classmates, friends, and family or the daily onslaught of negative news in our world. Also, most of us have experienced losing it and later (when we came to our senses) regretting the things we said or the way we behaved when our emotions got the best of us. As Aristotle (in *Nichomachean Ethics*) and Daniel Goleman (1995) noted, "Anyone can become angry—that is easy. But to be angry with the right person, to the right degree, at the right time, for the right purpose, and in the right way—that is not easy." God calls us to have self-control (2 Timothy 1:7) and to "not sin" in our anger (Ephesians 4:26; Proverbs 29:11).

Of course, God has much to say about our minds and thoughts. Here are a few examples (emphasis mine):

- Be transformed by the **renewing of your mind**. —Romans 12:2

- Love the Lord your God with all your heart and with all your soul and with all your mind and with all your strength. —Mark 12:30

- The end of the world is near. **You must be the boss** over your mind. Keep awake so you can pray. —1 Peter 4:7 (NLV)

- Be made new in the attitude of your **minds.** —Ephesians 4:23

- For as he **thinketh** in his heart, so is he. —Proverbs 23:7 (KJV)

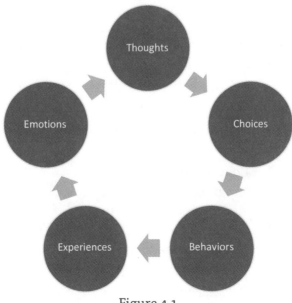

Figure 4.1

Along with neurologists, psychologists, cognitive behavior therapists, and many other researchers, Dr. Joe Dispenza (2018) informs us that the way we think has an impact on our lives. Our thoughts are intimately connected to our future and in many ways create or change our reality. We think about 60,000–70,000 thoughts in one day. Interestingly, 90% of those thoughts are the same thoughts as the day before. As our thoughts are connected to our lives, they create our choices. These repeated choices lead to our repeated behaviors. Our repeated behaviors create repeated experiences, and these experiences produce repeated emotions. These repeated emotions drive the same thoughts. It is a cycle. Our biology, neurocircuitry, neurochemistry, neural hormones, and even our genetic expression play a major role in how we think, how we act, and how we feel. How we think, act, and feel is called our personality (Dispenza, 2018). Our personality creates our personal reality. "That is how emotional learning becomes ingrained; as experiences are repeated over and over, the brain reflects them as strengthened pathways, neural habits to apply in times of duress, frustration, hurt" (Goleman, p. 263).

Reflection:
What is the progression for creating our personal reality?

_____

_____

_____

Where in this progression can you envision spiritual decisions that would transform (Romans 12:2-3) your personal reality?

_____

_____

_____

The NLP Model of Communication
Neuro linguistic programming (NLP) is a tool we can use to renew our minds and transform our lives (Romans 12:2). This model incorporates three significant components involved in producing human experience: neurology, language, and programming. NLP teaches us that one can use the language of the mind to consistently achieve specific and desired outcomes. God created our mind, body, emotions, and nervous system (Psalm 139:13–15). NLP allows us to take more control of these processes.

Our nervous or neurological system coordinates our body's actions by transmitting signals to and from different parts of the body. Linguistics is the scientific study of language and involves an analysis of its form, meaning, and context. Language determines how we interact and communicate with others. Our programming is how we internally represent our experiences—our habitual thoughts, feelings, reactions, beliefs, and traditions. These internal representations (sometimes called tapes) run our bodies and behavior. Programming refers to our ability to utilize these internal representations (in our neurological system) to change our mind and body states to achieve our desired outcomes. To the extent that these processes and mechanisms lie outside our awareness, they control us. Increasing awareness, competency, flexibility, and knowledge of mental and cognitive processes improves our ability to excel.

Bodenhamer & Hall (1996) note that NLP also emphasizes modeling or replicating excellence. As Christianity is about modeling Jesus, the integration of NLP and faith can deepen our relationship with God and improve discipleship efforts. NLP provides tools that allow us to strive for excellence, internalize empowering beliefs, control how we think, feel, and behave, and remove any past emotions or limitations that hinder personal transformation. NLP will allow you to take captive every thought and make it obedient to Christ (2 Corinthians 10:5).

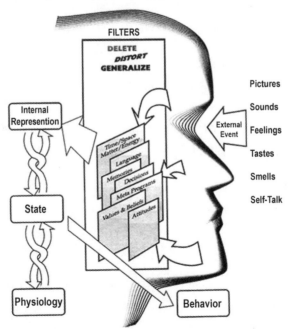

Figure 4.2 – NLP Model of Communication (James, n.d.)

Coming to understand the NLP model of communication has transformed my life in several fantastic ways. As seen on the left side of Figure 4.2, science informs us that our emotional state impacts and is intertwined with our physiology and our internal representations (see also Figure 3.1). Our internal representations (or cognitions) are how we make sense of the world. With information coming at us from pictures, sounds, feelings, tastes, smells, and our self-talk (right side of Figure 4.2) at about 400 billion bits per second, we must filter all that we receive. Thus, our God-given filters include our brain's ability to delete, distort, and generalize information (top of Figure 4.2). Our filters also include our subconscious attitudes, values, beliefs, meta programs, decisions, memories, language, time/space, and matter/energy. We conduct this filtering **unconsciously.** The NLP Model of Communication helps us understand how our internal representations, emotional state, and physiology all lead to our behavior (bottom of Figure 4.2). In *Emotional Intelligence,* Goleman (1995) also notes that thoughts are associated in the mind not just by content, but also by mood (p. 73).

Internal or mental representations are a presentation of the mind in the form of an idea or image (vocabulary.com). Internal representations are considered cognitive content—the sum or range of what has been perceived, discovered, or learned. We create internal representations when we, through our senses, represent what's happening outside us (pictures, sounds, feelings, tastes, smells, and self-talk) to ourselves internally. These representations or interpretations are also called evaluations. Typically, we are not consciously deciding the beliefs, values, attitudes, and memories we have. We acquire all these unconscious filters throughout life. Our current internal representations (how we interpret the world) are being influenced by these filters, which are typically outside our conscious awareness. Imagine our mental fortitude when we bring these subconscious filters to our awareness, to our conscious minds. Imagine how we can further optimize our spirituality, relationships, and lives with greater EQ skills (conscious awareness)!

Reflection:

Metacognition is defined as "awareness and understanding of one's own thought processes" (Lexico, 2019). How much have you thought about your thinking? Your internal representations? Have you had any repeated thoughts about or made any evaluations of your thinking?

_____

_____

_____

Our emotional state and physiology are so completely connected that a positive mood brings to our remembrance positive memories, and a negative mood (anger, fear, hurt, guilt, anxiety, worry, sadness, etc.) causes us to recall more challenging memories. Researchers have found that mild mood changes affect our thinking. This is all the more reason why God implores us to think about whatever is true, noble, right, pure, lovely, admirable, excellent, or praiseworthy (Philippians 4:8). Imagine what a daily habit of such godly thinking could produce! **We can choose which neural circuits we repeatedly wire together as we consciously recall that they fire together. Let's keep the Philippians 4 thoughts firing!**

Reflection:

Have you ever observed the ripple effect of your emotions and moods—the primary drivers of your behavior (Bradberry & Greaves, 2009)? Have you ever asked others how they are affected by your emotions?

_____

_____

_____

Additionally, emotional arousal shows up physiologically—most apparent are autonomic activations. Dr. John Gottman notes that even before we have some awareness of our emotions, there can be physiological indications. "Emotions and motor behavior are inextricably linked" (Purves, 2001). With your emotions or the emotions of others (like joy, hope, inspiration, serenity, gratitude, anger, sadness, fear, hurt, and guilt) have you ever noticed any of these changes:

- Increases or decreases in heart rate
- Changes in blood flow (blushing or turning pale)
- Piloerection—hair standing up
- Sweating
- Gastrointestinal motility and indigestion

- Body temperature changes
- Changes in breathing
- Trembling lips
- Weakened limbs
- Crying
- Increased adrenaline (racing heart, shaking limbs, shallow breathing, widening eyes)
- Fainting
- Muscle tension
- Changes in voice and tone (flattening or heightened)
- Clenching of teeth or fists
- Dry mouth
- Fidgeting
- Eyebrows raised
- Moving back/away
- Looking away
- Relaxation
- Smiling
- Fatigue
- Headache
- Back problems/pain
- Rash

Many of the aspects of our autonomic nervous system emotional responses are beyond our conscious control. It is amazing that God created our brains and bodies to effectively handle every situation with which we are faced.

As early as the late 1980s, Aaron Beck, the founder of cognitive and cognitive behavioral therapies, noted that the real emotional exchange in relationships is shaped by our thoughts. In addition, "Those thoughts, in turn, are determined by another, deeper layer, which Beck calls 'automatic thoughts'—fleeting, background assumptions about oneself and the people in one's life that reflect our deepest emotional attitudes" (Goleman, 1995, p. 137). These internal representations affect every area of our lives and determine our behavior.

Even more notable is the scientific finding that our brains are so powerful that **once a distressing thought becomes automatic it can become self-confirming.** Our filters look for what will confirm our thoughts and ignore or discount anything that would question or disconfirm that view. "These thoughts are powerful; they trip the neural alarm system" (Goleman, 1995, p. 137). These thoughts can also trigger emotional hijackings where we get stuck ruminating about whatever confirms our viewpoint. Imagine having the clear-mindedness and self-control (EQ's self-management) that leads to getting stuck with positive thoughts versus seeing things through negative lenses. With the right information and tools (see Chapter 10) we can do just that. With a greater understanding of how our mind works, we can "create our own future" as we and God desire!

Reflection:

What are the three filters we use to handle the information coming into our minds from pictures, sounds, feelings, tastes, smells, and even self-talk (see Figure 4.2)? What experiences (positive and negative) come to mind as you think about these three filters in your personal life and the lives of those in your circles of influence?

_____

_____

_____

_____

_____

What are your thoughts on the interdependence of our internal representations, emotional state, and physiology? How do you see this interdependence playing out for good in your life? How have you seen this interdependence playing out in unhealthy ways in your life?

_____

_____

_____

Based on the NLP model of communication (Figure 4.2), what drives/determines our behavior? Which of the three components would you most like to optimize more fully?

_____

_____

_____

How much control do you believe you have over your internal representations, emotional state (states of depression, anxiety, happiness, serenity, etc.), and physiology?

_____

_____

_____

What scriptures can you use to back up your beliefs about your level of control over your internal representations, emotional state, and physiology?

_____

_____

_____

_____

_____

_____

We Feel It First – The Physical Pathway for EQ

God wants us to be competent and thoroughly equipped for every good work (2 Timothy 3:17). Thus we need to understand how our brain operates. With awareness, knowledge, and EQ skills, we can better maximize brain functioning. Bradberry and Greaves (2009) note that "the daily challenge of dealing effectively with emotions is critical to the human condition because our brains are hard-wired to give emotions the upper hand" (p. 6).

All senses travel through our bodies in the form of electrical signals. All external events (pictures, sounds, feelings, tastes, smells, and self-talk) enter our brain at its base near the spinal cord (Figure 4.3). These electrical signals then travel through the limbic system of our brain, where we feel. This is where emotions are produced. Only after the signals travel through the limbic system do they reach the prefrontal cortex where rational or logical thinking takes place. This is the scientific rationale for counting to ten before reacting or responding. We need to give our brain time for the rational thinking to catch up with the emotions. "The communication between your emotional and rational 'brains' is the physical source of emotional intelligence" (Bradberry & Greaves, 2009, p. 7).

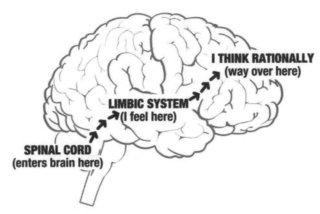

Figure 4.3 – Physical Pathway for EQ
Emotional Intelligence 2.0 (Bradberry & Greaves, 2009, p. 7)

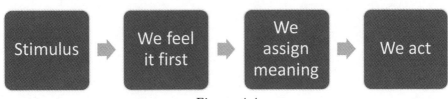

Figure 4.4

Figures 4.3 and 4.4 illustrate the science of EQ. By understanding how we feel the stimulus first and need time for our rational brain to kick in, we can better manage our emotions. We can have greater self-control (Galatians 5:22–23; 2 Timothy 1:7; 2 Peter 1:5–7).

Reflection:

How would counting to 10 (and counting back to 0 if necessary) be helpful for you when you are emotionally triggered by some stimulus?

_____

_____

_____

Regarding godly relationships (1 Corinthians 12:12–27), our brains are also wired to provide a continual analysis of information through our senses to decide how and when to initiate and be open to connection with each other (Boeder, 2017). As humans, we have the capacity to sense threat at its most subtle levels, beyond logic or cognition. This deeply wired system is firing whether we want it to or not (Boeder 2017). The beauty of a nervous system that helps us survive life-threatening events is that it also supports us in deepening our feelings of closeness and connection with one another (Boeder, 2017). "The more we understand how our bodies play a role in our relationships, the more we can make them work for us instead of against us" (Boeder, 2017).

_____ **Chapter Four – Part I Summary** _____

This chapter included a large amount of information. Great job combing through it! In order to internalize what you have read and reflected upon, please select the **three main points** that resonated with you.

To anchor your **top three learnings** or (new or deepened) convictions, list them here:

_____

_____

_____

Record your **one SMART decision** here:

_____

_____

_____

Part II – Optimize Your Mind

Now that we understand a few basics about our mind and how it works, we will explore how we can better optimize God's amazing gift. With increased knowledge, awareness, and skills (competence), we can increase self-control. We can more fully master our minds!

The Power of Our Neuroplastic Brain

Scientific research has shown us that by the time we "are 35 years old, we become a set of memorized behaviors, unconscious habits, automatic emotional reactions, beliefs, and perceptions and even attitudes that function like a computer program" (Dispenza, n.d.). The repetition of actions conditions our bodies and our mind/brain. We largely function unconsciously. **Ninety-five percent "of most people's behaviors, attitudes, thoughts, beliefs, and emotional reactions are subconscious programs"** (Dispenza, n.d.). These subconscious programs are like old cassette tapes or a playlist stuck in a constant loop, in our minds.

Yet one of the most encouraging facts about the brain, to me, is that we can consistently shape and even change our neural circuitry! Our brains, no matter our age, have neuroplasticity. That means that our magnificent brain can reorganize or restructure itself by forming new neural connections throughout life. We can rewire our brain to adapt to various environments. We can even reset our internal representations and eliminate toxic emotional residue connected to past events (Chapter 10). One of my favorite memes (credited to Dr. Joe Dispenza) is that "a memory without the emotional charge is called wisdom." God wants us to live in accordance with wisdom (Proverbs 2:6) as opposed to being driven by any inappropriate or unwarranted emotions and limiting beliefs.

Goleman (1995) notes that the underlying basis for our level of EQ "is, no doubt, neural, but as we will see, the brain is remarkably plastic, constantly learning. Lapses in emotional skills can be remedied" (p. 44). The four core EQ skills represent habits and responses that, with the right effort, can be improved on. Even though our internal representations and filters are subconscious, they are not outside our control. Our brains create neural networks that remain the same and become hardwired if there are no attempts to create new networks or change the neural circuitry. Brain research (Goleman, 1995) has demonstrated that our thoughts and emotions become self-fulfilling prophecies. Neurons and thoughts that fire together wire together. We can build our brain's neural networks with negative thoughts and moods or with godly and positive thoughts.

I remember being constantly reminded, when I was a teacher and administrator, of the Pygmalion or Rosenthal effect. Educators were encouraged to believe the best of all our students, since what we believed about them and their aptitude was likely to become their reality. Studies have shown time and again that self-fulfilling prophecies exist—that what we believe can become the reality. Since nerve cells that fire together wire together, our neural circuits become more connected. Over time, our brain becomes hardwired. We can make daily decisions on the thoughts that we use to build our neural circuits. We can expect our lives to change (John 10:10) when we think the same godly thoughts, make the same godly choices, demonstrate the same godly behaviors, and reproduce the same godly experiences that produce the same healthy emotions (Figure 4.1), which stamp the same networks of neurons into the same pattern. We can hardwire our brains for God!

As we strive to increase our spiritual maturity, emotional health, and godliness, every time we learn something new, we create new synaptic connections. Learning is making new connections. Amen that as disciples we are committed to continual growth into the likeness of Christ (2 Corinthians 3:18). Nobel Prize laureate Eric Kandel (2000) found that when we learn one bit of information, we double the connections in our brain from 1,300 to 2,600. When we continue to learn, information that is promptly reviewed, repeated, and remembered creates new neural networks/circuits. Thus, Joe Dispenza (n.d.) notes that learning is making new synaptic connections, and remembering can be seen as maintaining and sustaining connections.

God calls us to leave the past behind and to strain or press on toward the goal ahead (Philippians 3:13–14). We can create our desired future and be defined by our vision of our future or we can be defined by the recorded and unconscious memories and patterns of our past. If not defined by a passionate vision bigger than ourselves, our old hardware of the past, in our brains, controls our predictable lives (Dispenza, n.d.).

Joe Dispenza (n.d.) notes that to truly change is to think greater than our situation. Our external environment turns on different circuits in our brain, causing our thinking to be equal to everything we currently know. We will need to think beyond our environment, our life circumstances, and the conditions in our world if we are to continue growing and see God's kingdom come. Every person who greatly impacted the world was able to see beyond the present circumstances and envision a better world. Individuals like Mother Teresa, Dr. Martin Luther King, Jr., and Nelson Mandela thought greater than, or beyond, their current environment. Jesus also modeled this ability as He focused on the joy set before Him (Hebrews 12:2). Each moment we stop making the same choices that we always make, we will be uncomfortable, but we will be heading toward our new self—toward greater spiritual maturity and EQ. Our brain can change, and therefore our lives can change. We can decide on the thoughts, choices, behaviors, experiences, and emotions (Figure 4.1) on which we will build neural connections. With that said, we can and must allow God to really change/transform our minds (Romans 12:2)!

Reflection:

What kind of future do you want to create? What vision will you keep alive in your mind? Will the thoughts of your mind support this future or repeat the predictable choices, behaviors, experiences, and emotions of the past?

_____

_____

_____

Ninety to ninety-five percent of our daily lives is run by subconscious programs. Which subconscious programs (tapes) are most salient in your life? Which of these tapes are evident to those around you? Are your programs, thoughts, and behaviors centered primarily on your relationship with God?

_____

_____

_____

What "self-fulfilling prophecies" have you seen become realities? How will you begin to live as if the future reality you envision is present in the moment?

_____

_____

_____

Our Conscious and Unconscious Minds

God created each part of our brain (Genesis 1:26). Before learning about NLP, I had never really considered the differences between my conscious and unconscious minds. Yet, throughout history, many philosophers, preachers, teachers, researchers, biologists, and psychologists have provided helpful information on our conscious and unconscious minds. We are considered to be the sum of our conscious and unconscious thoughts, emotions, and beliefs. God says, "For as he thinketh in his heart, so is he" Proverbs 23:7 (KJV). Our unconscious mind is like a tape recorder. It has recorded everything, even the things that happened when we were in utero. Freud informed us that much of our emotional lives are unconscious and that "feelings that stir within us do not always cross the threshold into awareness" (Goleman, 1995, p. 54). Goleman also notes that "any emotion can be—and often is—unconscious. The physiological beginnings of an emotion typically occur before a person is consciously aware of the feeling itself" (p. 54). If preconscious emotions become strong enough, they can break into our awareness—into our conscious minds.

> The moment of an emotion coming into awareness marks its registering as such in the frontal cortex [of the brain]. Emotions that simmer beneath the threshold of awareness can have a powerful impact on how we perceive and react, even though we have no idea they are at work. (Goleman, 1995, p. 55)

Once we are consciously aware of our thoughts, emotions, and beliefs, only then can we evaluate them and make decisions about them. "In this way emotional self-awareness is the building block" (Goleman, p. 55) for the other three EQ skills and for our ability to live the lives that God has planned for us (Hebrews 13:20–21).

As I learned more about NLP and Time Line Therapy®, the role of our unconscious mind stood out to me. I was amazed! I had never thought about what my unconscious mind was doing. I had no clue that most of what is going on with me (body functions, thoughts, feelings, behavior, interactions, etc.) is unconscious. We can think of these two parts of our mind like those of an iceberg (Figure 4.5). Envision that beneath the surface is our unconscious mind and programming. You have probably heard people talk about the "tapes" playing in our heads. That is our subconscious or unconscious mind. The tip of the iceberg above the surface would be our conscious mind and choices.

Figure 4.5

Our unconscious mind is the part of our mind that we are not consciously aware of right now. For instance, we are typically not aware of our feet touching the floor and our back touching the chair, the air we are breathing, our eyes blinking, our heart beating, and all the noises happening around us. Wikipedia (2019) provides helpful information, reporting that the term "unconscious mind" was developed in the 18th century and stating, "The unconscious mind consists of the processes in the mind which occur automatically and are not available to introspection, and include thought processes, memories, interests, and motivations."

NLP trainers all over the world teach the following about the role (or prime directives, rules, commands) of our unconscious mind (Tad James, 2018):

1. **Stores memories**

2. Organizes all memories—makes associations; categorizes

3. Represses memories with unresolved negative emotional charges—sometimes called emotional baggage, where we can currently or in the future relive our past because of "baggage"

4. Presents repressed memories for resolution—to make rational decisions and to release emotion

5. Runs the body—automatically runs basic physical functions based on blueprints

6. May keep the repressed emotions repressed for protection

7. Preserves the body

8. **Is the domain of the emotions—the part of us that feels**

9. Is a highly moral being—accepting the morality we've been taught and have accepted

10. Enjoys serving, needs clear orders to follow—needs to be consistent

11. Controls and maintains all perceptions—the ability to perceive can be increased

12. Generates, stores, distributes, and transmits energy—energy can be increased

13. Maintains instincts and generates habits

14. Needs repetition until a habit is installed

15. Is programmed to continually seek more and more—there is always more to discover

16. Functions best as a whole, integrated unit—incongruences need to be integrated

17. Is symbolic—uses and responds to symbols

18. Takes everything personally—the basis of "perception is projection"

19. Works on the principle of least effort—path of least resistance

20. Does not process negatives—omits the "not" in "do not fall"; needs positively worded statements (e.g., "watch your step")

Reflection:

What roles/prime directives of our unconscious minds stand out to you the most? Why? How can this knowledge help you transform and mature spiritually and emotionally?

_____

_____

_____

_____

The extent that our conscious and unconscious processes and mechanisms lie outside our awareness is the extent to which they control unconscious processes. In addition, optimal learning and change is considered to happen unconsciously or in tandem with our unconscious mind. Frequently, good intentions are not enough for achieving our desired outcomes and goals. "Any kind of learning is unlikely to occur effectively without the interaction between prior knowledge and cognitive abilities, and the emotional and motivational states of learners" (Kuldas, 2013, p. 6). Yet God always comes through with good news! In Hebrews 9:14, He tells us, "How much more, then, will the blood of Christ, who through the eternal Spirit offered himself unblemished to God, cleanse our consciences from acts that lead to death, so that we may serve the living God!" We can retrain our emotional circuitry for our own good and God's glory! Additional details on how we use our unconscious mind to rewire our neural circuitry is in Chapter 10.

Brain Waves

Pertinent to the ability to master our minds, our brains and brain development are absolutely fascinating. The more we know about our brain, the better we can manage it and use it to optimize our emotional states, transform our internal representations, and manage our behavior. "At the root of all our thoughts, emotions, and behaviors is the communication between neurons within our brains" (Brainworks, n.d.). The electrical impulses that happen within neurons and when our neurons communicate with each other are called brain waves or neural oscillations.

Our brain experiences five different types of brain waves, and each has a normal frequency range in which it operates. Each type of brain wave controls a variety of states of consciousness, ranging from a deep dreamless sleep to high mental activity. All the brain waves work simultaneously, and the dominant brain wave determines our current state of mind.

The brain wave entrainment site Itsu Sync (n.d.) notes that "everything in our daily lives—from stress, poor diet, lack of exercise, trauma, pollution, the environment, and more—causes our brain waves to become unbalanced." Our optimal state is when our brain waves fall within normal ranges and we feel relaxed, sharp, clear minded, energetic, focused, and happy. We feel fantastic. So my question is always, how do we get to such a state? Table 4.1 provides some of the major functions/capacities for each of our brain wave levels.

Brain Wave Function and Capacity – Table 4.1

Age of Development	Brain Wave	FUNCTION, CAPACITY & EFFECT
Birth–2	*Delta*	—Lowest and slow frequency —Improved memory, subconscious learning, problem solving, and language retention —Deep, restful, dreamless sleep —Loss of body and external awareness —Complete and profound relaxation —Feeling of calmness and euphoria —Reduction of pain, headaches, anger, and irritability —Deepest state of hypnosis or meditation —Healing and regeneration stimulated
2–6	*Theta*	—Subconscious; reduced consciousness —Suggestible, programmable state —Brain picks up skills and learns by observing —Downloading a high volume of information into subconscious memory —Brain wave state in hypnosis —Deep/induced meditation/relaxation and introspection —REM sleep – dreaming —State of unconscious problem solving —Increased long-term memory, focus, creativity peace, emotional healing, and motivation —Decreased mental fatigue, procrastination, fear, absent-mindedness —Twilight state—as we wake or go to sleep —Where we hold our emotions, history, and nightmares

6 +	Alpha	—Calm consciousness states and mental stability—the brain's resting state —Ideal condition to learn new information, keep facts, perform elaborate tasks, learn languages, and analyze complex situations —Less susceptible to outside programming —Reduced stress and anxiety —Awareness of self and purpose —Calm/relaxed yet alert state—bridging conscious mind and unconscious mind —Creative thought and ability to memorize or absorb without active concentration —Grounded; being "present" —Feelings of satisfaction (similar to those from addictions) —Increased serotonin, mood elevation, arousal, and clarity —Subconscious correlation —Daydreaming, lucid state, intuition, visualization —Meditation and relaxation activities/exercises enable alpha state; mind/body integration
12 +	Beta	—Significant progress in memory, reading, spelling, math, and planning —Release of growth hormone for muscle development and rejuvenation or recovery —Most used brain rhythm —Tremendous amount of energy required —Normal waking state of consciousness, active thought process, and alert/attentive mental activity —Active or focused consciousness, processing, learning, concentration, problem-solving, decision-making, arousal, and cognition —Busy/fast thinking —Experience euphoria and ecstasy like runners with serotonin release

		—Enhanced vigor and alertness —Ideal meditation and energy frequency for releasing stress —The emotional spectrum where self-control and emotional intelligence can be improved —Christ consciousness—develop empathy, spiritual practices, and identity
Varies	*Gamma*	—Fastest brain waves—above the frequency of neuronal firing —Peak performance state enhancing other frequencies —Less specific—simultaneous processing of information from different brain areas —Includes intelligence, focus, memorization, concentration, perception, problem solving, and consciousness —Does not exist alone, but with other brain wave states —Grouping of stimuli into a coherent whole —Requires a quiet mind

Brainworks (n.d.), Itsu Sync (n.d.), Wikipedia (2019)

Brainwave information helps us to better understand the different states in which our brains operate. "Our brainwave profile and our daily experience of the world are inseparable. When our brainwaves are out of balance, there will be corresponding problems in our emotional or neuro-physical health" (Brainworks, n.d.). Over- or under-arousal of brain activity is connected to anxiety/worry, depression, negativity, motivation, libido problems, hypervigilance, impulsiveness, poor judgment/insight, autism, nerve pain or spasticity, attention deficits, procrastination, memory or learning challenges, and chronic pain (Brainworks, n.d. & Amen, 2005). Instabilities in brain rhythms correlate with issues such as obsessive-compulsive disorder, aggressive or explosive behavior, anger, panic attacks, bipolar disorder, migraines, epilepsy, sleep apnea, anorexia/bulimia, diabetes, lack of empathy, and addictions (Brainworks, n.d. & Amen, 2005). Thus, Dr. Daniel Amen has famously noted that if we change our brain, we can change our lives!

With knowledge about our brains, we can learn to work toward getting into our desired states of mind. Any issue with our health is connected to our brain functioning. Dr. Joe Dispenza claims that after a 1986 biking accident that left him paralyzed, his healing was largely due to his Creator and harnessing the power of thought (Schomer, Morrissey & Noonan, 2017). He notes that "thoughts are the language of the brain and feelings are the language of the body" (Dispenza, 2019). How we think and feel creates our state of being. For instance, in my post-counseling degree training, we were privileged to be taught "the learning state," which helped me when I took my mental health counselor licensing exam after only three weeks of study. I was able to focus and retain more with this practice. Also, in Time Line Therapy® (discussed in Chapter 10), theta brainwaves are dominant and the harmful residue of emotions and limiting beliefs/ decisions connected to past events can be eliminated. In Qi Gong, a standard medical technique in China used for cultivating and balancing chi (life energy), alpha brainwaves are dominant. Additional methods of altering our perceptions and brainwaves include meditation, yoga, PEMF, neurofeedback, and brain wave entrainment. We can harness the power of God's creation—our brain and its processes (1 Peter 1:13)!

Reflection:

What do you now know (that you didn't before) about your brain that will help you to better manage your everyday life, emotions, and relationships?

_____

_____

_____

_____

_____

Into which brain wave states would you like to enter more often? Delta, where there is complete relaxation? Theta, where long-term memory, focus, and peace are heightened? Alpha, where there is reduced stress and anxiety?

_____

_____

_____

Paul's Comments on Our Brains

When I think about how our brains work, I also think of the way Paul described our struggles in Romans 7. To get a better understanding of the intended meaning of a writer's message, I frequently review different versions of the same scripture. In verse 23 Paul notes:

Romans 7:23	Bible Version
But I see another law at work in me, waging war against the law of my mind and making me a prisoner of the law of sin at work within me.	NIV
When I come up against the Law I want to do good, but in practice I do evil. My conscious mind whole-heartedly endorses the Law, yet I observe an entirely different principle at work in my nature. This is in continual conflict with my conscious attitude, and makes me an unwilling prisoner to the law of sin and death.	PHILLIPS
But there is something else deep within me, in my lower nature, that is at war with my mind and wins the fight and makes me a slave to the sin that is still within me In my mind I want to be God's willing servant, but instead I find myself still enslaved to sin.	The Living Bible
It happens so regularly that it's predictable. The moment I decide to do good, sin is there to trip me up. I truly delight in God's commands, but it's pretty obvious that not all of me joins in that delight. Parts of me covertly rebel, and just when I least expect it, they take charge.	The Message

What also stood out to me with Romans 7:23 was the way the different translations recorded the phrases for "law," "at work in me," "waging war against," and especially, "law of my mind."

Law – additional Bible translations:

- Law and rule of action (AMP)

- A different standard or another power (EXB)
- A different principle (ISV)
- God's commands (MSG)
- Power (NLT)
- Decree (OJB)

At work in me – additional Bible translations:
- In the members of my body [in appetites and desires] (AMP)
- In the sensitive appetites and wills of the flesh (AMPC)
- In my members (BRG)
- In the parts of my body (CSB)
- In my body (CEB)
- In every part of me (CEV)
- Working in my outward actions (EXB)
- At work deep inside of me (NLV)
- In my limbs and organs (NTE)
- In my natural capacities (OJB)
- Operating in my humanity (TPT)

Waging war against – additional Bible translations:
- Fighting against (CEV)
- Warring in opposition to (DARBY)
- Makes war against (ERV)
- Rebelling against (GNV)
- Fights with my mind (NLV)
- Battling against (TLV)

Law of my mind – additional Bible translations:
- My reason (AMPC)
- The law that my mind accepts (ERV)
- Standards that my mind accepts (EXB)
- Standards my mind sets (GW)
- Law which my mind approves of (GNT)
- The moral principles of my conscience (TPT)

In addition, Paul closes out Romans 7 stating,

What a wretched man I am! Who will rescue me from this body that is subject to death? Thanks be to God, who delivers me through Jesus Christ our Lord! So then, I myself in my mind am a slave to God's law, but in my sinful nature a slave to the law of sin. (vv. 24–25)

Paul is describing a profound conflict that every Christian finds inherent in their life in Christ: Christ dwells in them (Galatians 2:20), yet sin also dwells in them (Romans 7:17, 20). Perfect conformity to God's will is, at present, out of reach. Salvation has "already" and "not yet" dimensions (Ligonier Ministries, n.d.). Though God calls us to ever increase our knowledge (2 Peter 1:3–11), we still need to rely on Him for salvation.

Reflection:

What does Romans 7:23 tell us about our mind, conscience, subconscious mind, sin, and God's word? What terminology struck you most? Why?

_____

_____

_____

_____

_____

_____

How is Romans 7:23 helpful as we work toward better managing the emotional, conscious, and unconscious parts of our brain?

_____

_____

_____

_____

What helps you to navigate the spiritual reality of our "already" and "not yet" salvation?

_____

_____

_____

The Brain and Our Relationships

The field of social neuroscience has grown at a rate that is hard for relationship experts and psychologists to keep up with. The researchers now know that our brain is a social organ that evolves. Relationships actually build our brains. More specifically, though we don't usually consider our brain when we think of developing godly relationships, it is imperative that we do! Our brain is where we:

> Perceive, understand, remember, evaluate, desire, and respond to people. The somewhat bizarre fact of life is that the people who are in our lives are not simply who they are. They are some interesting mix of who they are and what we make of them in our brains. If we understand the ways in which relationships impact our brains, we can likely change our brains to alter the ways in which we interact with others too. (Pillay, S. 2018)

Simply understanding our brain's automatic reactions of attachment, transference, emotional contagion, compassion, mindfulness, and cognitive empathy can help us to better navigate and deepen relationships. Keep in mind that we live in constant relationship to others and we impact each other's ability to regulate our social and emotional behavior. Understanding how our brain exists in relationship to other brains helps us to better understand ourselves and other human beings.

Since there are countless books and research articles available, it is impossible to dive into all these areas, but I hope that you will be inspired to learn more about how relationships shape your brain and how your brain shapes your relationships. I will briefly note three topics on which we can take some immediate action—EQ, safety, and self-confirming stimulus. First, when we better understand how our brain/mind works, we can better implement and practice the self-awareness, self-management, social awareness, and relationship management strategies offered in *Emotional Intelligence 2.0* (Bradberry & Greaves, 2009). When we understand the workings of our mind, we can learn to master our EQ skills by beginning with Bradberry & Greaves' first strategy of not treating our emotions/feelings as good or bad! Since our brain records everything, we really have to watch our evaluations, as they are messages to our unconscious minds.

There are a number of things that could help us reduce negative judgments about our emotions and the emotions of others, if only we knew more about how our brain operates—how it develops, grows, connects, learns, and heals. I have heard (and repeated) some of the following unfortunate statements even from well-meaning Christians:

- I/you shouldn't be sad.

- I/you shouldn't be angry or feel hurt.

- I/you shouldn't feel worried or anxious.

- I/you shouldn't be so emotional.

- I/you should be happy.

- I/you don't have any emotions.

- I'm not sure what I feel about this situation.

- I/you shouldn't feel angry with God.

Let's work at not treating our emotions and feelings nor those of others as good or bad. In addition,

> The latest research in neurobiology shows that emotional safety is one of the most important aspects of a satisfying connection in a loving relationship. We need to feel safe before we're able to be vulnerable. As Brené Brown reminds us, "Vulnerability is the birthplace of love, belonging, joy, courage, empathy, accountability, and authenticity." (Boeder, 2017)

> Stephen Porges, Ph.D., a pioneer in the field of neuroscience and one of the world's leading experts on the autonomic nervous system, confirms that we have an imperative for safety deeply wired into our minds and bodies. Porges' Polyvagal Theory describes how our autonomic nervous system mediates safety, trust, and intimacy through a subsystem he calls the social engagement system. Our brain is constantly detecting through our senses whether we are in a situation that is safe, dangerous, or life threatening. When our body and mind experience safety, our social engagement system enables us to collaborate, listen, empathize, and connect, as well as be creative, innovative, and bold in our thinking and ideas. This has positive benefits for our relationships as well as our lives in general. (Boeder, 2017)

We can watch for situations in which our emotions are hijacked or in which we are dealing with individuals that may not be "safe" at the moment. For further information, I frequently recommend Cloud and Townsend's book *Safe People*.

There is also a possibly detrimental "neutral dynamic in the mind that makes stereotypes of all kinds self-confirming" (Goleman, 1995, p. 157). Our brain works in such a way that we remember things that support our beliefs and discount things that challenge or do not support our current beliefs. Thank God that, even though we may have ungodly and unloving thoughts and beliefs traveling through our brains, we can decide how we will act in each situation. With knowledge about how our brain works, we can better manage our thoughts, emotions, stereotypes, relationships, and behavior! As we become more self-aware, we may reach a level of awareness where we can challenge ourselves to recognize stereotypes, implicit biases, and prejudices along with any emotionally charged beliefs that are not in line with God's word.

Reflection:

What additional brain research would you like to do regarding emotions, personality, evolution (our brain's ability to change), and our conscious and unconscious minds?

_____

_____

_____

The illiterate of the 21st century will not be those who cannot read and write, but those who cannot learn, unlearn, and relearn.

—Alvin Toffler

_____ Chapter Four – Part II Summary _____

This chapter included an immense amount of information. Great job combing through it! In order to internalize what you have read and reflected upon, please select the **three main points** that resonated with you.

To anchor your **top three learnings** or (new or deepened) convictions, list them here:

_____

_____

_____

Record your **one SMART decision** here:

_____

_____

_____

God, Trauma, and EQ – Linda's Testimony

I have been a big proponent of emotional intelligence for the last 30 years. I started with talk therapy after the tragic suicide of my father. This traumatic event also led me to read many self-growth books. Through therapy, I realized not only that I needed to deal with the emotional residuals of living through the suicide of a loved one, but also how growing up in a dysfunctional household affected me deeply. Even after I became a Christian and had the Bible as my main source of wisdom, there were still unwanted emotions and beliefs that needed to be addressed, like low self-esteem, a lack of trust, depression, and unforgiveness. I understood that God wanted to heal me and to use tools such as education, books, workshops, and therapy in my healing process.

There are many things over which we have little to no control. Yet I have found it to be empowering to take charge of my emotional health and healing. I was excited to take the Mastering Emotional Intelligence® workshop that Cresenda facilitated. I was impacted by the fact that when we receive signals in our brains, we feel it first (Figure 4.3). Then the signals move to the rational part of our brain; thus the recommended EQ strategy of counting to ten before we respond. It was great to learn the science behind it. I now see that I have more control in my life when I choose. We are also able to use EQ tools to help others once we become educated on how emotions work in our mind, body, and spirit—it's all connected.

We all have past hurts, and some of us have experienced seemingly unspeakable tragedies. Being educated and doing the work is necessary and a wonderful path to freedom. The benefits are priceless. It is another gift that God gives us!

Chapter Five

The Cost of Repressing Emotions

God expresses emotions of joy, disappointment, sorrow, grief, love, anger, jealousy, compassion, delight, desire, fear, hurt, guilt, peace, depression, pain, agony, exhaustion, disgust, empathy, forgiveness, and more. Jesus vividly expressed similar emotions in the Gospels. David, John, Jeremiah, Paul, Peter, and Elijah all did as well. I, on the other hand, attempted to ignore my emotions for most of my early life up until my college years. There was just too much sadness with my parents separating and divorcing, and my mother remarrying. There were additional challenges and traumatic events also. In my first book (Jones, 2014), I discussed in detail the different ways we can attempt to ignore and numb our emotions—addictions, relationships, busyness, service of and care for others, chaos, worry, exercising, sports, religion, approval of others, television, computer games, social networking, hobbies, work, codependency, and even the pursuit of success. The dictionary defines the word "repress" as keeping under control or suppressing; keeping down; putting down; quelling; and rejecting from our conscious mind (www. dictionary.com). There are immediate and long-term consequences of repressing our emotions.

Multiple areas of our lives are impacted when we stifle our emotions. Repressing our emotions is also harmful spiritually. I have been blessed to see a Pain Paradigm process work, in which those with pain above their waist can have that pain completely and quickly eliminated. As unbelievable as it sounds, it is miraculous each time I see or facilitate that process! As noted in Figure 3.1, our internal representations, emotional state, and physiology are connected. Thus, when we suppress our emotions, they can show up in our thinking and physiology. The Pain Paradigm process capitalizes on these connections to eliminate pain. Which of the following have been present in your life in the last six months?

Physical Symptoms
- ☐ Headaches
- ☐ Fainting Spells/Dizziness
- ☐ No Appetite/Overeating
- ☐ Stomach/Bowel Disturbances

☐ Palpitations
☐ Tremors – Shaking
☐ Poor Sleep
☐ Nightmares/Night Tremors
☐ Unusual Bodily Sensations
☐ Sexual Problems
☐ Tired/No Energy

Emotional Symptoms
☐ Anxiety
☐ Depression
☐ Self-Esteem Issues
☐ Fears/Worries
☐ Inferiority Feelings
☐ Panic Attacks
☐ Anger Issues
☐ Feeling Tense/Stressed
☐ Shyness/Loneliness/Isolation
☐ Poor Decision-Making
☐ Lack of Ambition or Interests
☐ Unable to Relax

Addictions
☐ Drinking Problem
☐ Drug Abuse
☐ Gambling
☐ Sexual/Pornography Addiction
☐ Food Addiction
☐ Excessive Shopping

Mental Health
☐ Mental Disorders
☐ Suicide Attempts
☐ Suicidal Ideas
☐ Visual Hallucinations
☐ Hearing Voices
☐ Disturbing Thoughts or Fears
☐ Mania

In addition to physical, emotional, and mental health symptoms and addictions, repressed emotions can show up and wreak havoc in our school, work, financial, social, and family lives. As a result of unexamined and ill-managed emotions, we even see violence, murder, suicide, crime, unwanted pregnancies, and emotional, physical, and sexual abuse.

I have been thinking about why some of us, followers of Christ, can desire to repress and ignore our emotions. Of course, the reasons for doing so are different, layered, and deep (Proverbs 20:5) for each of us. There are those among us who feel that we should only feel "positive emotions" (possibly out of gratitude) since we have been saved and will be with God in heaven. Others do not want to feel (or go back in time and relive) the horrible feelings—we just do not want to feel the pain. Some of us have even become aware of the fact that our emotions were not accepted (let alone validated) during our childhoods and have decided to continue with that way of living. Many of us subconsciously believe that anger and even sadness are wrong and sinful. Some of us are intellectually aware that emotions are just emotions and are not sinful in themselves, but still, based on poor models, we feel or believe that emotions are "bad." We are somehow capable of rejecting the humanity that God created in each of us.

To be clear, unless someone has a psychopathic or sociopathic personality, all humans have emotions. Psychologists have labeled those who do not know and are unable to put into words what they are feeling as alexithymics. Though we can all feel numb at times, an alexithymic lacks the fundamental skill of emotional intelligence: self-awareness. Goleman (1995) reminds us that our values are connected with our emotions and we will have faulty reasoning if we are not aware of our emotions.

Unfortunately, as mentioned before, many of us did not have healthy models for recognizing, understanding, and managing (RUM – Chapter Three Part I) our emotions. The discussion of EQ was not even a consideration for most until after Daniel Goleman published *Emotional Intelligence* in 1995. Understanding how our emotions create our behaviors, beliefs, and even decisions is also new to many of us (Figure 4.2). Regrettably, many men have been culturally (and subconsciously) trained to not appreciate, embrace, or display the emotional part of their being.

In our "toxic masculine culture," men are not supposed to show or even have any emotions. Most men have been conditioned to be task oriented, to suppress emotions, and to show the emotional part of themselves solely with their spouse or significant other. Despite work by countless legal and education advocates, the cost of our toxic masculine culture (Elliott, 2018) includes gender inequality, bias, and violence. While most men do not sexually assault or harass women, "most women (e.g., athletes, executives, researchers, and artists) experience it, fear it, and/or learn to adjust their behavior to avoid it—another symptom of the cultural sickness" (Elliott, p. 18). This repression of emotion has had calamitous impacts on our society. Our emotions will seep out (or even explode) no matter how hard or unconsciously we try to ignore them.

Meanwhile, boys and girls are taught very different lessons about experiencing, recognizing, understanding, and handling emotions. Harvard's Carol Gilligan points to "a key disparity between the sexes: boys take pride in a lone, tough-minded independence and autonomy, while girls see themselves as part of a web of connectedness" (Goleman, 1995, p. 131).

> As Deborah Tannen has pointed out in her book *You Just Don't Understand*, these differing perspectives mean that men and women want and expect very different things out of a conversation, with men content to talk about 'things,' while women seek emotional connection. (Goleman, p. 132)

These contrasts in schooling in the emotions foster very different skills, with girls becoming more "adept at reading both verbal and nonverbal emotional signals, at expressing and communicating their feelings," and boys becoming adept at "minimizing emotions having to do with vulnerability, guilt, fear and hurt" (Goleman, p. 132).

We each have to decide whether our culture—independent of where we live in the world—or the Bible will be our standard (as Christians) for how we handle our emotions and the emotions of others. In John 13:34–35, Jesus is clear on what God calls us to be and do: "A new command I give you: Love one another. As I have loved you, so you must love one another. By this everyone will know that you are my disciples, if you love one another." Brené Brown has researched vulnerability for many years. She has published many books and shared her findings and life in TED talks—see "The Power of Vulnerability" and a Netflix video entitled *The Call to Courage*. She informs us that we cannot expect to enjoy the positive emotions if we attempt to ignore the more challenging ones. If we try to cut off a part of ourselves, we will cut off more of ourselves. Suppressing our feelings is like marking "return to sender" on God's good gift (Mahaney, 2017).

Though we may have heard the opposite, **time does not heal all wounds.** We have to intentionally work on specific, measurable, attainable, relevant, and timely (SMART) goals in order to see the transformation referred to in Romans 12:2 and the "life to the full" referred to in John 10:10 that God desires for us, our relationship with Him, and our relationships with ourselves and others. For emotional health, healing, intelligence, and freedom, we must face our emotions. We can be emotionally mature if we effectively deal with emotions such as anger, sadness, fear, hurt, and guilt.

Yale researchers note that intense negative emotionality (warranted and appropriate or not) of any kind (such as anger, hostility, anxiety, and depression) that sends stress hormones through our bodies raises our blood pressure, sickens us, impedes medical recovery, and heightens our risk of death from heart disease (Goleman, 1995). Tad James Co. (2018) notes that toxic emotional residue is not safe for the body. Inappropriate anger has been found to lead to heart attacks and heightened cholesterol. Unwarranted sadness can weaken our immune systems and lead to depression. Residual fear can end up in excessive stress, post-traumatic stress disorder, and phobias. Lingering guilt lowers our energy, and conflict can lead to cancer (Tad James Co., 2018). We now know that chronic emotional stress is harmful. The medical findings do not mean that we should suppress emotions, but that if we want to live healthy spiritual lives, we must learn to effectively manage these everyday emotions. Building EQ skills does just that. We can learn to effectively handle stress and all the other emotions that can challenge our minds, bodies, and souls.

The good news is that schools and organizations have awakened to the fact that intelligence, performance, and production alone will not get us to our personal and collective goals. Schools and many organizations have realized that emotional intelligence is needed for success, leadership, and peak performance. Schools have implemented social and emotional learning (SEL) or character education curricula. Fortune 500 companies are now training employees on EQ. Individuals are also awakening to the fact that with EQ skills—self-awareness, self-management, social awareness, and relationship management—they can better attain their goals and have fun while doing so. As practically as helping people make an average of $29,000 more per year (Bradberry & Greaves, 2009), EQ has an amazingly positive impact.

The additional good news is that God's loving commands are extremely helpful. In Philippians 4:8 we are given specific instructions: "Finally, brothers and sisters, whatever is true, whatever is noble, whatever is right, whatever is pure, whatever is lovely, whatever is admirable—if anything is excellent or praiseworthy—think about such things." We know that inappropriate residual emotions can have a toxic impact on us. God knew that positive thoughts and affirmative emotions can be a tonic (Figure 4.2). God has also gifted us with tools such as Time Line Therapy® (Chapter 9), meditation, yoga, exercise, healthy diets, and mindfulness that can help us to tap into the power of His Spirit and the fruit of the Spirit as listed in Galatians 5:22–25.

We need as many spiritually, physically, and emotionally healthy disciples on and able to work the harvest fields! Our emotional intelligence determines just how spiritual, intimate with God, and fruitful for God it is possible for us to be. With EQ, "as psychoanalyst Harry Stack Sullivan pointed out, we learn how to negotiate intimate relations—to work out differences and share our deepest feelings" (Goleman, 1995, p. 251). We need all those skills for a great relationship with God and others. With working on developing EQ skills of self-awareness, self-management/control, social awareness, and relationship management, there is hope for all of us to be able to walk with God as He desires and help many others to do the same. With our biblical foundation intact, social and emotional competencies can make all the difference. This has been a growth journey for me, and I hope you will join the journey!

_____ Chapter Five Summary _____

To internalize what you have read and reflected upon in Chapter Five, please select the **three main points** that resonated with you.

To anchor your *top three learnings* or (new or deepened) convictions, list them here:

_____

_____

_____

Record your **one SMART decision** here:

_____

_____

_____

God, Emotions, and Emotional Intelligence

The fruit of the Spirit is love, joy, peace, forbearance, kindness, good-
ness, faithfulness, gentleness and self-control.
—Galatians 5:22–23

Love is patient, love is kind. It does not envy, it does not boast, it is not
proud. It does not dishonor others, it is not self-seeking, it is not easily
angered, it keeps no record of wrongs. Love does not delight in evil
but rejoices with the truth. It always protects, always trusts, always
hopes, always perseveres. Love never fails.
—1 Corinthians 13:4–8

Above all else, guard your heart,
for everything you do flows from it.
—Proverbs 4:23

I am deeply grateful that God amazingly gave us His word so that we can know Him, understand how to be saved, and know how to walk with Him! I am also grateful that the Bible is a window into the hearts of the authors, God, and Jesus. Their hearts are consistently revealed. Their emotions are laid bare for us to experience and empathize with them, and even so that we can consider whom we should model our lives and emotional intelligence after—our self-awareness, self-management, social awareness, and relationship management. The Bible provides direction that promotes healthy intrapersonal and interpersonal functioning. At the same time, "the Bible has little to say, however, about the actual nature and functioning of emotions. Thus, this information has to be constructed from theology and implications of biblical passages or from extra-biblical sources" (Campbell & Bufford, 2012, p. 1). God is the source of our emotions, as we are made in His image (Genesis 1:27).

Unlike EQ growth efforts in business or in one's personal life independent of a Christian worldview, we have the ideal model (Jesus) and we have the Holy Spirit's power! God said that we, His creation, are good (Genesis 1:31), and we are called to be transformed into His likeness (2 Corinthians 3:18; Ephesians 4:15; Romans 8:29). Therefore, we aspire to have an emotional life like that of our Lord and Savior Jesus Christ! Jesus was our model of "personal presence, self-control, emotional expressiveness, and discernment of situations" (Edmiston, 2001, p. 6). As we strive to be more like Jesus was emotionally, we can transform the areas of our lives that are out of balance or not matured. With our decision to make Jesus Lord, our emotions need to be sanctified just as do all the other aspects of our lives. It is comforting and inspiring to know that we are promised the ability to be inwardly renewed day by day (2 Corinthians 4:16).

With Figure 3.1, we discussed how our internal representations, emotional state, and physiology are connected, but we did not yet fully focus on where God is in the picture. As you already know, our spirituality is interdependent with our thoughts, emotions, and physical state. If we are determined to be pessimists, it will be close to impossible to think (Philippians 4:8) and live (Galatians 5:22–25) spiritually the way God has called us to. If we refuse to live in accordance with godly principles in the Bible, our emotional, mental, and physical state will be negatively impacted. On the other hand, as much as it is up to us, when we choose to live the way our omnipotent God has designed, we will experience peace and blessings beyond what we could ever ask or imagine (Ephesians 3:20). It is our choice.

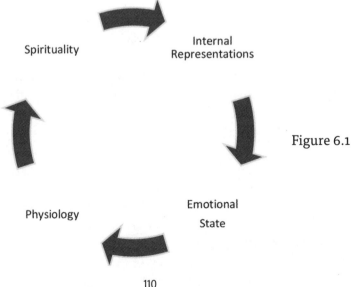

Spirituality

Internal Representations

Figure 6.1

Physiology

Emotional State

Just as we are more likely to get angry when we are tired or hungry, we are likely to have more positive thoughts and emotions when we are walking closely with God and Jesus is Lord of every area of our lives. Note that competent therapists are trained to **address the biological, psychological, social, and spiritual aspects of clients' lives because treatment plans and outcomes are dependent on the clients' health in each of those areas.** God calls and empowers us to sanctify all these areas of our lives (1 Corinthians 6:11). We are called to live by the Spirit, put to death the misdeeds of the body (Romans 8:13), and walk by the Spirit (Galatians 5:16). Amen that the Spirit who raised Jesus from the dead renews us and gives us sanctification power! "The goal of biblical EQ is fellowship with God" (Edmiston, 2001, p. 17).

Emotional Functioning

Emotions provide us with information about ourselves and others. They give us the ability to have intimate connections with others and our motivational system (Campbell & Bufford, 2012). Even more helpful, our emotions can "serve us by giving us vital information that helps us react to and cope with our environment" (Campbell & Bufford, p. 2). Most helpful is that our emotions promote a more complete relationship with God in which we are equipped "to better comprehend, appreciate, and serve God" (Campbell & Bufford, p. 2).

Before the Fall (Genesis 3), our thoughts, emotions, and behavior were all congruent. After the Fall, with the impact of sin, we now are living with distorted, unwarranted, and inappropriately experienced and expressed emotions. We know full well that we cannot always trust our emotions (Jeremiah 17:9). The Fall has led to our emotions causing confusion, interpersonal alienation, chaos, projection, and sin (Campbell & Bufford, 2012). Our emotions, if our spirituality and EQ skills are not intact, disrupt our relationships with God, ourselves, and others. Eckman (n.d.) importantly notes that our external relationships are but a reflection of what is going on within (Proverbs 4:23; Matthew 12:34; Colossians 3:8–11). Through the Bible, God has given us great examples to follow or imitate and of the detriment of life without EQ.

Good or Bad Emotions?

Bradberry & Greaves (2009) encourage us to quit treating our feelings as good or bad. In contradiction, Sam Williams (2011) posits that the belief that emotions are neither good nor bad, but just are, is a pernicious myth. Edmiston (2001) breaks emotions down into three classes: holy, human, and fleshly. Campbell & Bufford (2012) make the case that primary emotions are amoral and "secondary emotions involve conscious volitional actions" (p. 7). In addition, Christian teachers have repeatedly admonished listeners to not "follow emotions." So, what are we to believe as we strive to live by God's word, be godly, and imitate Christ—to be spiritually transformed and emotionally intelligent?

Varying theories and perspectives can be complicated, yet I believe that we can glean at least some sensible guidance from the wealth of information published by researchers, writers, and believers about emotions. Many have published opinions about anthropomorphism and the idea that human emotions are theomorphic. We usually consider hate to be a "bad emotion," but God hates evil, and we are called to do the same. I also think of possibly confusing biblical directives to hate sin and to hate our mother, brother, sister, etc. (Luke 14:26). We are also called to wholeheartedly love God and our neighbors. The love of Jesus demonstrated by His sacrifice on the cross (Romans 5:8) is not the typical warm and gooey feeling we consider when we think about the emotion of love, yet Jesus' sacrifice was the ultimate display of love. We really must be critical thinkers as we continue on our road to spiritual maturity and greater EQ.

A review of the research and discussions with Christian teachers has led me to largely agree with the theory that our primary (immediate, spontaneous, respondent, and involuntary) emotions are amoral. What is important in relation to emotional intelligence and spiritual maturity is Campbell & Bufford's (2012) report that "our responses to or expression of these emotions may be either moral or immoral" (p. 7). **Our conscious decisions (or choice points) regarding our emotions are what we are responsible for.** We can choose what we will do with feelings and emotions when they arise. We can choose to focus on the negative or the positive. We can choose joy and peace as opposed to nursing grudges, fueling anger, or bitterness. We at times psych ourselves up or attempt to cool ourselves down. "It is our volitional actions (intentions, motivations)" that carry moral weight (Campbell & Bufford, p. 8). Where we can improve our emotional intelligence and increase our spiritual maturity is in our efforts to increase our conscious deliberation before responding to our emotions.

In the Time Line Therapy® process (Chapter 9), which subconsciously eliminates damaging emotional residue and limiting beliefs/decisions connected to past events, one requirement is that we watch our evaluations, as they are indeed messages to our unconscious minds. As you recall, our unconscious minds record everything. Thus, it would be more beneficial for us not to judge our emotions nor to attach "good" or "bad" labels to them. Without the judgment, we can allow ourselves to better recognize, understand, and manage (RUM) our emotions as opposed to burying the initial (primary) emotions under all the emotions that are attached to any negative judgments. Without judgment, we can allow God to use our emotions as "alarms"—notifying us that something is important and should be addressed (Bradberry & Greaves, 2009). Not only can we increase our conscious awareness of our emotional responses, but with current neurological tools, we can also rewire our subconscious tapes and replace destructive emotional residue with positive learnings for ourselves and our future!

Jesus' Emotions

Christ is an amazing model of emotional functioning. He has been the only person on earth with congruence of emotion, thoughts, behavior, and experience (Campbell & Bufford, 2012). Campbell and Bufford also note that "Christ experienced and expressed perfect (accurate and adaptive) emotions" (p. 3). Jesus also "did not engage in emotional denial, repression, or projection" (Campbell & Bufford, p. 4). We have all likely heard the term "emotional baggage." Since He was willing to express a full range of emotions and since there was a completeness to His emotional expression, Jesus did not have emotional baggage. With pure motives and appropriate responses, "the manifestation of His emotions accomplished righteous purposes" (Campbell & Bufford). Jesus displayed no less than miraculous emotional authority, effectiveness and power as He withstood enormous pressure and persecution (Edmiston, 2001). Jesus was always poised.

Though there are a myriad of examples, the following are a few of Jesus' emotions and feelings noted in the Bible:

1. Alone/abandoned/hurt/pain—Matthew 26:40–46; John 6:15; Matthew 27:46—on the cross

2. Amazement/marveled/surprised/astonished—Matthew 8:10—faith of the centurion

3. Anger/deep distress/frustration—Mark 3:5—Pharisees' cruelty; Mark 11:15–18—God's house turned into a den of robbers; Matthew 23:33; Matthew 17:14–20; Mark 4:35–41

4. Calm/peace—Mark 4:35–41—in the storm; Matthew 26:47–50—when arrested

5. Compassion/concern—emotion recorded the most in the gospels—Matthew 9:36; 11:28–30; 15:32; Matthew 14:14; 20:34; Luke 7:13; Mark 6:34; 8:2; John 8:1–11; Hebrews 4:15; John 19:25–27

6. Connected (loved and loving)—Lazarus, Mary, Martha, Peter, James, John; friend of sinners

7. Desperation/passion—Hebrews 5:7—prayed with loud cries and tears

8. Gratitude—gave thanks at meals—recorded nine times

9. Joy – Luke 10:21—after sending out the 72; Matthew 18:11–13—parable of restoring the one of 99; John 15:10–11, 17:13—Jesus notes His joy; Hebrews 12:2

10. Love—Mark 10:21—rich young ruler; John 20:2; 1 John 4:19–21; Ephesians 3:18

11. Mixed or conflicting emotions of sorrow, trouble, and joy—Mark 14:32–62; Hebrews 12:2

12. Pain/grief/agony/discouragement—Matthew 27:34–54; Luke 22:42–44—on the cross; Mark 7:34, 8:12

13. Sadness/sorrow—Luke 19:41–42; John 11:33–38—Jesus wept; Isaiah 53:3; Matthew 27:46; Hebrews 5:7

14. Troubled in soul or spirit/fear—John 12:27, 13:21; Matthew 26:36–41; John 11:33, 38

15. Tired/fatigued—John 4:6; Matthew 14:13, Mark 6:31, Luke 5:16, John 6:15— withdrew

16. Zeal and disgust—John 2:13–17—for God's honor

17. Forgiveness—Luke 23:34

Reflection:

Which of Jesus' emotions are easy for you to recognize and understand?

_____

_____

_____

Which of Jesus' emotions are more difficult for you to recognize and understand?

_____

_____

_____

In your personal life, which of Jesus' emotions are more difficult for you to except, experience, recognize, understand, and manage (RUM)?

_____

_____

_____

_____

_____

_____

The Power of the Holy Spirit

Of course, we will not be completely transformed into the likeness of Christ (2 Corinthians 3:18) until we leave this earth. "Come, Lord Jesus!" Yet we have God's Holy Spirit to help us now in our efforts to build our EQ skills and live as close to the life of Jesus as we can. In the meantime, we can rely on the Holy Spirt and capitalize on the wisdom that God promised (James 1:5).

God calls us to love Him with all our heart, soul, mind, and strength (Mark 12:30). Jesus was our model in that He "perceived life's situations with His Spirit," "was moved on the basis of those perceptions," and "candidly expressed His emotions to those closest to Him" (Edmiston, 2001, p. 23). Jesus was our RUM model. He recognized or perceived His own emotions. He understood His emotions. And lastly, He effectively expressed and managed His emotions. Romans 8:11 ensures us that we have power through God's Spirit: "And if the Spirit of him who raised Jesus from the dead is living in you, he who raised Christ from the dead will also give life to your mortal bodies because of his Spirit who lives in you."

David Eckman (n.d.) writes about how the Holy Spirit is given to believers to profoundly influence and enrich our emotional lives. Note through the following scriptures how Jesus, our model, referred to His own soul and spirit (Edmiston, p. 23):

- **Matthew 26:38**—Then he said to them, "My soul is overwhelmed with sorrow to the point of death. Stay here and keep watch with me."

- **Matthew 27:50**—And when Jesus had cried out again in a loud voice, he gave up his spirit.

- **Mark 2:8**—Immediately Jesus knew in his spirit that this was what they were thinking in their hearts, and he said to them, "Why are you thinking these things?"

- **Mark 8:12**—He groaned *and* sighed deeply in His spirit and said, "Why does this generation demand a sign? I assure you *and* most solemnly say to you, no sign will be given to this generation!" (AMPC)

- **Mark 14:34**—"My soul is overwhelmed with sorrow to the point of death," he said to them. "Stay here and keep watch."

- **Luke 10:21**—At that time Jesus, full of joy through the Holy Spirit, said, "I praise you, Father, Lord of heaven and earth, because you have hidden these things from the wise and learned, and revealed them to little children. Yes, Father, for this is what you were pleased to do."

- **Luke 23:46**—Jesus called out with a loud voice, "Father, into your hands I commit my spirit." When he had said this, he breathed his last.

- **John 11:33**—When Jesus saw her weeping, and the Jews who had come along with her also weeping, he was deeply moved in spirit and troubled.

- **John 12:27**—"Now my soul is troubled, and what shall I say? 'Father, save me from this hour'? No, it was for this very reason I came to this hour."

> - **John 13:21**—After he had said this, Jesus was troubled in spirit and testified, "Very truly I tell you, one of you is going to betray me."
> - **John 19:30**—When he had received the drink, Jesus said, "It is finished." With that, he bowed his head and gave up his spirit.

Through our relationship with God, we can experience and express our emotions in godly ways, as Christ exemplifies. More specifically, when we are spiritually and emotionally mature, our "emotions are informative, supportive, spontaneous, and expressed appropriately" (Campbell & Buford, 2012. p. 6). Campbell and Bufford also note that, as we imitate how Christ lived with His emotions, allow the Holy Spirit to lead us, and work out our salvation (Philippians 2:12), we are empowered to:

1. Experience emotions accurately and adaptively
2. Allow emotions to aid us in decision-making
3. Have congruent emotions, thoughts, and actions
4. Have complete versus fragmented emotions
5. Express fully versus deny, repress, or externalize emotions; and
6. Express emotions with pure motives versus being manipulative or destructive.

Reflection:
In which of the six areas of emotional empowerment do you feel your EQ skills are glorifying God?

_____

_____

_____

In which of the six areas of emotional empowerment do you feel you need to increase your EQ skills?

_____

_____

_____

Love and the Fruit of the Holy Spirit

There may not be any better biblical descriptions of or equivalents to the results of a healthy EQ than Paul's description of love in 1 Corinthians 13:4–8 and of walking by the Spirit and having the fruit of the Spirit in Galatians 5:13–26. Paul gives us a clear image of what it means to live a life by the Spirit and the opposite, to live in accordance with our sinful nature. We know that the fruit of the Spirit is "love, joy, peace, forbearance, kindness, goodness, faithfulness, gentleness and self-control" (vv. 22–23).

As discussed in the previous section, Jesus was in tune with and in control of His spirit. The fruit of the Spirit is exemplified in Jesus' life, and we also want the fruit to permeate our lives. 1 Corinthians 13 (discussed in more detail in Chapters 3 and 7) describes how we are to be like Jesus in our patience, kindness, contentment, humility, meekness, honor (the dignity of others), concern for others, forgiveness, love of what is good and true, protection, trust, hope, and perseverance. The four core EQ skills of self-awareness, self-management, social awareness, and relationship management correlate with what God has called us to in the two amazing and challenging passages mentioned above.

Reflection:

Which descriptors of love and the Holy Spirit's fruit correlate with the EQ skill of self-awareness?

_____

_____

_____

Which descriptors of love and the Holy Spirit's fruit correlate with the EQ skill of self-management?

_____

_____

_____

Which descriptors of love and the Holy Spirit's fruit correlate with the EQ skill of social awareness?

_____

_____

_____

_____

Which descriptors of love and the Holy Spirit's fruit correlate with the EQ skill of relationship management?

_____

_____

_____

_____

God's Emotions

God has emotions, which He expresses and shares. It would be good for us to do all we can to live in His image since we are made in His image (Genesis 1:26–28). As previously noted, in most cultures, men are expected to suppress and ignore emotions (other than anger) in order to be respected. Additionally, in many cultures, women are not allowed to or are not supposed to feel sadness, grief, or anger. Ironically, women are diagnosed with depression nearly twice as much as men. Since Jesus and God express varied emotions and are vulnerable and intimately connected to others, our goal is to reflect their holiness. Though we are flawed, God's emotions are perfect and holy. In the Bible, God expresses anger, compassion, sorrow, joy, and more. Though many more are implied from His actions, here are just a few examples of God's emotions in the Bible:

1. Anger/wrath—Psalm 106:40; Isaiah 5:25; Ezekiel 34; Psalm 2:5; Jeremiah 7:18–19

2. Love—John 3:16; Romans 5:8

3. Hate/disgust/disdain—Psalm 5:5; Psalm 11:5; Psalm 2:4; Deuteronomy 16:21–22; Ezekiel 34

4. Compassion—Genesis 19:16; Exodus 33:19

5. Grief—Genesis 6:6; Isaiah 53:3, 63:10; Psalm 78:40

6. Joy/delight—Nehemiah 8:10; Zephaniah 3:17; Isaiah 42:1, 62:5, 65:19

7. Forgiveness—John 3:16

Reflection:

Do any of God's emotions surprise you? Are any of the emotions typically not ascribed to God in our culture today? Are any of God's emotions hard for you to understand or accept?

_____

_____

_____

Is God's anger and wrath like the human anger and wrath you have seen in yourself, your family, at school, or at work? Do you hate the things that God hates and love the things that God loves?

_____

_____

_____

Is God's love and compassion like the human love and compassion you have seen in your family, at school, or at work? Is your love and compassion like God's?

_____

_____

_____

David and Emotional Intelligence

We cannot talk about emotions and emotional intelligence without mentioning David. David was considered the person whose heart was nearest to God (Acts 13:22). He expressed his love more than anyone through his writings. The Psalms are exemplary for helping us be heart/gut-level real with ourselves, in our relationship with God, and in expressing our humanity through our emotions. David and the other psalmists displayed a myriad of emotions. David's EQ included high levels of self-actualization, self-regard, emotional expression, interpersonal relationships, and problem solving (Branson, n.d.). Though we read that David had issues with self-awareness (2 Samuel 12) and impulse control (his dealings with Bathsheba and Uriah), he was considered to be a man who was humble, reverent, trusting, devoted, faithful, obedient, and repentant. Those are all great EQ skills.

For example, in Psalm 30, Edmiston (2001) observes the following about the display of David's emotional life:

- Emotions were temporary

- Emotions were resolved righteously

- Emotions were directed toward God

- A wide range of emotions was displayed

- God was seen in the midst of each situation

- Emotions were not suppressed

- False perspectives and beliefs were changed; and

- "In the expression of emotions there is genuine dignity and beauty" (p. 34).

In another example, Gaultiere (n.d.) notes that we see David's optimistic emotions and laments in Psalm 55. David talks about trouble, suffering, terrors, horrors, violence, strife, malice, abuse, the fear of God, war being in hearts, trust, care, and sustenance. Psalm 55 also shows David feeling anger, distraught, fear, trembling, longing, rest, confused, joy of fellowship, rage, distress, and manipulated. This psalm is a prayer and plea to God. The emotions jump off the page to the reader. David embraced his humanity (emotions), and God was pleased with the resulting level of intimacy.

God's Will for Emotional Intelligence

With strong EQ skills, we will not be tossed back and forth or blown here and there! God describes spiritual maturity in relation to the impact of our emotions in Ephesians 4:11–16 as follows:

> *So Christ himself gave the apostles, the prophets, the evangelists, the pastors and teachers, to equip his people for works of service, so that the body of Christ may be built up until we all reach unity in the faith and in the knowledge of the Son of God and become mature, attaining to the whole measure of the fullness of Christ.*
>
> *Then we will no longer be infants, tossed back and forth by the waves, and blown here and there by every wind of teaching and by the cunning and craftiness of people in their deceitful scheming. Instead, speaking the truth in love, we will grow to become in every respect the*

*mature body of him who is the head, that is, Christ. From him the whole
body, joined and held together by every supporting ligament, grows
and builds itself up in love, as each part does its work.*

God's will for emotional intelligence is that we build our EQ skills to
grow and become more spiritually mature. The Bible constantly addresses
the world of emotions (Eckman, n.d.). To be spiritually mature and
emotionally intelligent, we need to address our emotional world and the
emotional world of those in our lives. Chapters 9 and 10 will provide a
deeper dive into how we can better manage emotions, the importance of
focusing on what we desire, and the messages we send to our unconscious
mind. Let God be glorified in our ability to recognize, understand, and
manage (RUM) our emotions!

Reflection:

*In addition to Jesus, there are many Bible heroes who displayed amazing EQ skills.
Who else comes to mind as examples we can follow? How are they examples?*

_____

_____

_____

_____

_____

In which situations did individuals in the Bible display a lack of EQ skills?

_____

_____

_____

_____

*What emotions did Paul display? For some examples, see Acts 20:24; Romans 9:2;
Philippians 1:7-8, 13, 2:2, 17, 3:4-10, 4:11; 2 Corinthians 7:16, 12:7-11, 21; Colossians
3:12.*

_____

_____

_____

_____

_____

_____ **Chapter Six Summary** _____

To internalize what you have read and reflected upon in Chapter Six, please select the **three main points** that resonated with you.

To anchor your **top three learnings** or (new or deepened) convictions, list them here:

_____

_____

_____

Record your **one SMART decision** here:

_____

_____

_____

God, Spiritual Maturity, and EQ
—Heather's Testimony

My experiences over the past 7 to 10 years have revealed the absolute need for EQ in my life. Work pressures, marriage issues, challenges with children, and family dysfunction—all these circumstances posed great obstacles for me. My inability to define my feelings, much less work through them, prevented me from resolving situations like these effectively. Instead, I found myself on a perpetual rollercoaster that replicated the chaos of my childhood.

As a disciple of Christ, I wanted desperately to please God, but by reading scriptures alone, I was ill-equipped to move beyond my emotional immaturity. I also needed practical ways to approach situations and to define what was happening factually and emotionally. It was only through the help of individual, marriage, and group therapy that I became aware of and began to understand the options I had for responding and working through these circumstances.

Over the past several years, I have read many books, completed numerous workbooks, and attended multiple group sessions, which were all related to EQ in one way or another. I have been permitted to share my journey and learning by facilitating groups addressing *Healing for Damaged Emotions,* purity, and codependency. My life is markedly different because of this path. My marriage is much more authentic, my parenting much less enmeshed, and my leadership far more encouraging without removing responsibility. Regarding the dysfunction of my family of origin, I am at peace and praying for greater EQ for us all.

Psalm 20:1–2 states that God sends us support and help from his sanctuary so that we can navigate this journey with confidence. For me, God has provided wise and insightful people as a primary resource along with books and workshops that have aided in my understanding of myself and the emotions that have been gifted to me. EQ leads to a wholeness that we Christians can only benefit from.

If we desire to live life to the full as Jesus encourages us to (John 10:10), this work will be hard. It requires much determination, discipline, and passion to work through the rough patches and those fear-filled memories toward the ability to see life with undistorted vision. Remember, God is with you every step of the way and He will reveal more and more of Himself to you as you journey. It's a beautiful way to walk out the text as you walk with God—and grow in your emotional intelligence.

Chapter Seven

The Bible on the Four Core EQ Skills

The purposes of a person's heart are deep waters,
but one who has insight draws them out.
—Proverbs 20:5

As previously noted, God describes high EQ skills and the core godliness concepts when His inspired word discusses love (1 Corinthians 13:4–8) and the fruit of the Holy Spirit (Galatians 5:22–23). We are called to love the way God and Jesus love. We are called to be full of God's Holy Spirit—love, joy, peace, patience, kindness, gentleness, faithfulness, gentleness, and self-control. Proverbs 20:5 also encourages us to understand our own motivations and to discern the motivations of others. My dear wise friend, Fernando Alejandro, notes that learning to draw out the purposes of the heart (for ourselves and others) is how we grow in EQ.

I can guess that most of us have felt discouraged at one time or another when we have worked hard to please God and bring glory to Him, but fell short of His call. We frequently miss the mark. We will continue to do so, but with EQ strategies and a Time Line Therapy® transformation process, we can eliminate any toxic emotional residue and limiting beliefs/decisions connected to past events and be left with the wisdom and positive learnings for our future (Chapter 9). Unbeknownst to many of us, **these unwarranted and inappropriate lingering emotions, along with limiting beliefs/decisions, have fueled much of our ungodly behavior and spiritual struggles.**

On the other hand, can you imagine the freedom, peace, and clarity that God has designed for each of us (Philippians 4:7)? Can you visualize the peace and clarity God has for you? He has given us tools to attain these inner emotional states and godly mindsets. Imagine eliminating the plague of unwarranted and inappropriate emotional residue and limiting beliefs or tapes in our heads! God wants us to be men and women of emotional intelligence and spiritual maturity. He does not want us to be tossed here and there (Ephesians 4:14) by the negative tapes in our heads or the emotional sewage connected to past events. God not only describes His vision for our lives, but He provides powerful tools to help us realize walking in His amazing light! God has promised that we can have the wisdom (James 1:5) that remains when we eliminate the emotional charge connected to past events.

There are countless scriptures we can reference that implore us to grow in our emotional intelligence and spiritual maturity. Furthermore, in Chapter 8, I have compiled a list of scriptures for each of the 66 *Emotional Intelligence 2.0* EQ development strategies. Here, we will explore just a few striking scriptures related to emotional intelligence.

Proverbs 20:5

As I mentioned earlier, when I want to better understand what a Bible writer is attempting to communicate in a passage, I look up the verse on www.biblegateway.com and study/compare all of the available Bible translations. Since Proverbs 20:5 is a great representation of God's will for our emotional intelligence, below is listed additional terminology for "The purposes of a person's heart are deep waters, but one who has insight draws them out" (NIV). The ICB states Proverbs 20:5 as "Understanding a person's thoughts is as hard as getting water from a deep well. But someone with understanding can find the wisdom there."

Purposes of a person's heart (NIV)
- Counsel in the heart of man (KJ 21)
- A plan (motive, wise counsel) in the heart of a man (AMP)
- Advice...from the deep waters of the heart (CEB)
- The heart's real intentions (CJB)
- Someone's thoughts (CEV)
- Getting information from someone (ERV)
- People's thoughts [advice, purpose] (EXB)
- Motive in the human heart (GW)
- Purpose in the heart of a man (LEB)
- Good advice...within a counselor's heart (TLB)
- Knowing what is right (MSG)
- The purposes in the human mind (NRSV)
- The intent of a man's heart (TLV)
- The real motives (VOICE)

Deep waters (NIV)
- Water in a deep well (AMP)
- Deep as the ocean (CEV)
- Like a deep well [waters] (EXB)
- Deep within a person (VOICE)

One who has insight (NIV)
- A man of understanding (KJ21)
- A person with discernment (CJB)
- If you are smart (CEV)
- A wise man (DRA)
- Someone with understanding (EXB)
- A discerning person (ISV)
- A man of intelligence (JUB)
- A man of deep understanding (TPT)

Draws them out (NIV)
- You will discover them (CEV)
- Can find the wisdom there (EXB)
- Reveals them (ISV)
- Draws from the well within (MSG)
- Draw it forth (NABRE)
- Brings them out (NIRV)
- Gets it out (NLV)
- Drawing it out (TPT)
- Draw them up and expose them (VOICE)
- Draweth it up (YLT)

Reflection:
How and why is Proverbs 20:5 a great biblical representation of the four core EQ skills of self-awareness, self-management, social awareness, and relationship management?

_____

_____

_____

Which phrases help you to understand God's will for our emotional intelligence?

_____

_____

_____

How many questions do you typically ask about a situation before sharing your thoughts, opinions, advice, and scriptures? Do you intentionally draw out others and seek to thoroughly understand before offering your thoughts?

_____

_____

_____

How many questions do you think would be good to ask before sharing your thoughts, opinions, advice and scriptures? Why?

_____

_____

_____

Have you ever thought of just asking questions and allowing a loved one to come to their own convictions versus sharing your thoughts and ideas? Have you seen this modeled? How could such a listening and support strategy be beneficial?

_____

_____

_____

Galatians 5:22–26

Galatians 5:23–26 also describes those with high EQ skills of self-awareness, self-management, social awareness, and relationship management. The NIV states:

But the fruit of the Spirit is love, joy, peace, forbearance, kindness, goodness, faithfulness, gentleness, and self-control. Against such things there is no law. Those who belong to Christ Jesus have crucified the flesh with its passions and desires. Since we live by the Spirit, let us keep in step with the Spirit. Let us not become conceited, provoking and envying each other.

Amen that disciples have living in us the same Spirit that powerfully raised Jesus from the dead (Romans 8:11)! Let's continually learn HOW to allow God's Spirit to shine all the more vividly through us in this dark world! Here are additional terms from different translations of our Bible:

> **Love**—unselfish concern for others, loving, charity, affection for others, agape, divine love, unconditional love
>
> **Joy**—inner joy, gladness, happy, exuberance about life, joy that overflows
>
> **Peace**—peaceful, serenity, shalom, peace that subdues
>
> **Forbearance**—longsuffering, patience [not the ability to wait, but how we act while waiting], an even temper, patient, longanimity, tolerance, willingness to stick with things, not giving up, great-heartedness, patience that endures, long abiding
>
> **Kindness**—gentleness, benignity, sense of compassion in the heart, kindness in action, kindheartedness, good will
>
> **Goodness**—benevolence, generosity, conviction that basic holiness permeates things and people, a life full of virtue, mildness
>
> **Faithfulness**—fidelity, faith, loyal commitments, faith that prevails, being true
>
> **Gentleness**—tolerance, no need to force our way in life, gentleness of heart
>
> **Self-control**—able to marshal and direct our energies wisely, strength of spirit, keeping the body under control

Reflection:

Which terminology helps you to better grasp the meaning of the fruit of the Spirit? Which terms help you to build a better internal representation of how God wants to shine in/through our lives?

_____

_____

_____

You have taken the Emotional Intelligence 2.0 Appraisal®, reviewed your results, and selected one strategy of focus for each of three months. How well are the four core EQ skills showing up in your life through the Holy Spirit? Which fruit of God's Spirit is clearly evident in your life?

_____

_____

_____

Which fruit of the Spirit and which of the four core EQ skills need attention in your life? Do you recognize any parallels?

_____

_____

_____

In which movie clips (Emotional Intelligence 2.0 *Appraisal® resources) do you see people exhibiting the fruit of the Spirit?*

_____

_____

_____

1 Corinthians 13:4-8

1 Corinthians 13 also describes those who are spiritually mature and emotionally intelligent. Paul tells us:

> *Love is patient, love is kind. It does not envy, it does not boast, it is not proud. It does not dishonor others, it is not self-seeking, it is not easily angered, it keeps no record of wrongs. Love does not delight in evil but rejoices with the truth. It always protects, always trusts, always hopes, always perseveres. Love never fails.*

This description of love is similar to how we see God's Spirit in the lives of individuals. As we have seen, it is a great depiction of the four core EQ skills.

I vividly recall someone encouraging me to put my name in the place of love to reflect on how love is or is not showing up in my life. I always thought that I could just stop with the first description of love (patience) and have enough work for the rest of my life. I have seen a major change in my level of patience after completing the Time Line Therapy® transformation process. I think that this activity will continue to help me see how much I need God on a daily basis and how much I am grateful for His grace and love! Write your name in each of the blanks below. Take the time to read the phrases out loud.

_____ is patient.

_____ is kind.

_____ does not envy.

_____ does not boast.

_____ is not proud.

_____ does not dishonor others.

_____ is not self-seeking.

_____ is not easily angered.

_____ keeps no record of wrongs.

_____ does not delight in evil.

_____ rejoices with the truth.

_____ always protects.

_____ always trusts.

_____ always hopes.

_____ always perseveres.

_____ never fails.

Reflection:

How does it feel to describe yourself with each of the representations of love?

_____

_____

_____

How well are the four core EQ skills showing up in your life through 1 Corinthians 13 love? Which components of love are most clearly evident in your life?

_____

_____

_____

Which of the love descriptors and the four core EQ skills need attention in your life? Do you recognize any parallels?

_____

_____

_____

2 Peter 1:5–11

Lastly, for a general discussion on the four core EQ skills, my dear friends and admirable Bible students, Mark and Kenda Moloney, shared that 2 Peter 1:5–11 seems to aptly describe emotional intelligence. Peter writes to those of faith, to God's elect:

> *For this very reason, make every effort to add to your faith goodness; and to goodness, knowledge; and to knowledge, self-control; and to self-control, perseverance; and to perseverance, godliness; and to godliness, mutual affection; and to mutual affection, love. For if you possess these qualities in increasing measure, they will keep you from being ineffective and unproductive in your knowledge of our Lord Jesus Christ. But whoever does not have them is nearsighted and blind, forgetting that they have been cleansed from their past sins.*
>
> *Therefore, my brothers and sisters, make every effort to confirm your calling and election. For if you do these things, you will never stumble, and you will receive a rich welcome into the eternal kingdom of our Lord and Savior Jesus Christ.*

We see some of the same love and Holy Spirit terms that are in 1 Corinthians 13 and Galatians 5. We are called to confirm our calling and election. We are called to avoid a life without EQ—a life without love and the fruit of the Holy Spirit. We are called to possess these qualities in increasing measure and to make every effort. Once again, I am very grateful for the tools that God provides so that we will know HOW to do what He has called us to do and be who He has called us to be! For the sake of our own lives and the lives of our loved ones, I am asking that we develop greater capacity to see the hearts of others, to understand our own hearts, and to therefore be better equipped to move hearts closer to God. Not only does our salvation depend on our EQ capacity, but the salvation of those around us does too (1 Timothy 4:16). Teacher and author Douglas Jacoby has asked if we are primarily living in the frustration of Romans 7 or the freedom of Romans 8. Greater EQ and the tools discussed in this book can provide the freedom that we desire and all that God planned for our lives.

In 2 Peter 1:8, God says that if we possess these qualities in increasing measure, they will keep us from being ineffective and unproductive in our knowledge of our Lord Jesus Christ (NIV). For a deeper understanding, additional Bible versions use the following terminology:

In increasing measure—abound, increasing as you grow toward spiritual maturity, increasingly abound, growing in you, in abundance, keep growing, grow strong spiritually, building on what you've been given, continually increasing, describe you more and more, the more you grow like this, in plentiful supply, in abundant supply, multiply them, do these things more and more, overcome or be plenteous

Ineffective and unproductive—barren or unfruitful, useless and unproductive, inactive and unfruitful, not useful or meaningful, empty nor unfruitful, active and effective, complacent nor unproductive, of no use from having no fruit, inactive and fruitless, void nor without fruit, inert nor unfruitful, not idle nor unfruitful, never fail to be useful to God, living and productive, useful and fruitful, not wasting your time or failing to bear fruit

In 2 Peter 1:9, Peter also tells us: "But whoever does not have them is **nearsighted and blind,** forgetting that they have been cleansed from their past sins" (NIV). Our wealth of Bible translations provides greater insight with the following descriptions:

- Blind and cannot see afar off (KJ21)
- Blind, seeing only what is near (ASV)
- Blind, shortsighted [closing his spiritual eyes to the truth] (AMPC)
- Blind and groping (DRA)
- Cannot see clearly what they have (ERV)
- Can no longer see the reason why he was cleansed from his

former sins (PHILLIPS)

- Walks feeling the way with his hand (JUB)
- Can't see what's right before you, oblivious (MSG)
- Blind and has forgotten (NCV)
- Can't see very well (NIRV)
- Constantly closing his eyes to the mysteries of our faith (TPT)
- Can see only a little way (WE)
- Blind, dim-sighted (YLT)

Reflection:

Which terminology helps you to better grasp and internalize the importance of possessing godly qualities and EQ skills in increasing measure?

_____

_____

_____

Which terminology helps you to better grasp and internalize God's desire for us to be effective and productive?

_____

_____

_____

In your own words, describe the result of not having these qualities in increasing measure (v. 9)

_____

_____

_____

_____

Which terms help you to build a better internal representation of how God wants us to confirm our calling and election?

_____

_____

_____

Self-Awareness

As we noted, self-awareness is our ability to perceive our own emotions in the moment and understand our tendencies across situations (TalentSmart®, 2008). The Bible has a few things to say about self-awareness. God calls us to watch our life (1 Timothy 4:16); to not think of ourselves more highly than we ought, but with sober judgment (Romans 12:3); and to examine and test ourselves (2 Corinthians 13:5; Lamentations 3:40). Proverbs 21:2 informs us that we may think that our way is right but that God weighs what is in our hearts. David prayed that God would test, try, and examine his heart and mind (Psalm 26:2). Proverbs 14:8 tells us that the wisdom of the prudent is to discern their ways. 1 Timothy 3:9 calls us to hold to our faith with a clear conscience. Galatians 6:7 implores us to not be deceived, yet Jeremiah 17:9 informs us that our hearts are deceitful above all things and desperately wicked (KJV). All these scriptures speak to self-awareness, the foundation for the other EQ skills.

In addition, we can all have blind spots and thus we need each other. Proverbs 19:20 and 13:20 talk about how we are wise when we walk with and listen to the wise. Even more so, when we are not aware of our emotional wounds, we tend to bleed out on all those around us. **When we are not aware of our inner pain, we inflict it on others.** Self-awareness is required for emotional healing and emotional intelligence as well as happy and successful relationships. The greater our emotional awareness, health, and intelligence, the better decision makers we can be for God. More significantly, in Chapter 8, there are scriptures for each of the 15 self-awareness strategies to guide us on HOW to practically improve our self-awareness skills.

Reflection:

In which range was your EQ Appraisal® self-awareness score: a strength to capitalize on (90–100); a strength to build on (80–89); with a little improvement, this could be a strength (70–79); something you should work on (60–69); or a concern you must address (59 and below)? On which EQ strategy can you focus this month in order to increase your self-awareness skills?

_____

_____

_____

Self-Management

In our world of counterfeit "freedoms," living according to emotions (without rational thinking), being encouraged to trust and go with our heart, and the constant reports of incidents in which people are totally out of control, God provides the standard for self-discipline that is for our best interest and His glory. We have all heard people complain about Christians who do not act like Christ. Even Mahatma Gandhi is reported to have said, "I like your Christ; I do not like your Christians. Your Christians are so unlike your Christ." Self-control is required as we look to live life to the full (John 10:10), bear fruit (John 15), reap times of refreshing (Acts 3:19), and live the eternal life (John 3:16) that God desires and has designed for each of us.

The following are a few biblical translations of the concept of the term "self-control" as it is used in Proverbs 16:32: "Better a patient person than a warrior, one with self-control than one who takes a city" (NIV). Additional translations of the term "self-control" include:

- Ruleth his spirit – KJ21
- Rules and controls his own spirit – AMP
- Controlling one's emotions – CSB
- Controls his temper, rules his spirit – CJB
- Control your anger – ERV
- Controlling your temper – EXB
- Ruleth his own mind – GNV
- It is better to win control over yourself – GNT
- Rule their temper – NABRE
- Rule over your temper – TPT
- Lord of his soul, lord over himself – WYC

Reflection:

How do the other versions help you to understand God's will for our self-control skills? What stands out to you?

_____

_____

_____

Proverbs 25:28 (NIV)
> *Like a city whose walls are broken through*
> *is a person who lacks self-control.*

Additional biblical translations use the following terms for lack of self-control in this verse:

- Spirit is without restraint – ASV
- No self-control over his spirit – AMP
- Without self-control – CEB
- Cannot refrain his own spirit – DRA
- Cannot control themselves – ERV
- Unrestrained in spirit – EXB
- Refraineth not his appetite – GNV
- Cannot control your anger – GNT
- Does not control his temper – HCSB
- Does not control himself – ICB
- Spirit has no restraint – JUB
- Cannot rule his own spirit – NLV
- Live without restraint and are unable to control your temper – TPT
- Not refrain his spirit in/from speaking – WYC

Reflection:
How do the other versions help you to understand God's will for our self-control skills? What stands out to you?

_____

_____

_____

Acts 24:25

As Paul talked about righteousness, self-control and the judgment to come, Felix was afraid and said, "That's enough for now! You may leave. When I find it convenient, I will send for you."

Reflection:

How has fear shackled your personal life, self-control, family, leadership, fellowship? What would faith look like in these instances?

_____

_____

_____

_____

_____

_____

_____

_____

_____

1 Corinthians 7:5

Do not deprive each other except perhaps by mutual consent and for a time, so that you may devote yourselves to prayer. Then come together again so that Satan will not tempt you because of your lack of self-control.

1 Timothy 3:2

Now the overseer is to be above reproach, faithful to his wife, temperate, self-controlled, respectable, hospitable, [and] able to teach.

2 Timothy 3:1–5

But mark this: There will be terrible times in the last days. People will be lovers of themselves, lovers of money, boastful, proud, abusive, disobedient to their parents, ungrateful, unholy, without love, unforgiving, slanderous, without self-control, brutal, not lovers of the good, treacherous, rash, conceited, lovers of pleasure rather than lovers of God—having a form of godliness but denying its power. Have nothing to do with such people.

Reflection:
Based on the above scriptures, how can you better manifest God's will for self-control in your life?

_____

_____

_____

_____

_____

_____

In addition to the aforementioned scriptures, in Paul's letter to Titus, he includes self-control five times (NIV). The introduction in chapter 1 (verses 1–4) sets the stage for the topics he needed to discuss:

> *Paul, a servant of God and an apostle of Jesus Christ to further the faith of God's elect and their knowledge of the truth that leads to godliness— in the hope of eternal life, which God, who does not lie, promised before the beginning of time, and which now at his appointed season he has brought to light through the preaching entrusted to me by the command of God our Savior,*
> *To Titus, my true son in our common faith:*
> *Grace and peace from God the Father and Christ Jesus our Savior.*

As the NIV descriptive titles within Titus note, in three short chapters, Paul discusses appointing elders who love what is good, rebuking those who fail to do good, doing good for the sake of the gospel, and being saved in order to do good. Crete was known for laziness, gluttony, lying, and evil (*Life Application Bible*, 1991). Thus, Paul called for the Christians in Crete to be committed and self-disciplined servants. Paul also, and very importantly, addressed the character of leaders. Who we are is just as important as all the things we do. Paul instructs Titus to teach the disciples to live godly lives, to have healthy relationships, and to be good citizens. Paul's discipleship training included the need to be self-controlled. Please keep in mind that we can only effectively manage the things we are aware of. Self-control is not about ignoring, repressing, suppressing, or denying our emotions.

Titus 1:8

Rather, [the elder] must be hospitable, one who loves what is good, who is self-controlled, upright, holy and disciplined.

Titus 2:2

Teach the older men to be temperate, worthy of respect, self-controlled, and sound in faith, in love and in endurance.

Titus 2:3-5

Teach the older women.... Then they can urge the younger women...to be self-controlled and pure, to be busy at home, to be kind, and to be subject to their husbands, so that no one will malign the word of God.

Titus 2:6

Similarly, encourage the young men to be self-controlled.

Titus 2:11-13

For the grace of God has appeared that offers salvation to all people. It teaches us to say "No" to ungodliness and worldly passions, and to live self-controlled, upright and godly lives in this present age, while we wait for the blessed hope—the appearing of the glory of our great God and Savior, Jesus Christ.

Reflection:

Based on God's word, what new or deeper convictions have you gained regarding the EQ skill of self-management or self-control?

_____

_____

_____

In which range was your EQ Appraisal@ self-management score: a strength to capitalize on (90–100); a strength to build on (80–89); with a little improvement, this could be a strength (70–79); something you should work on (60–69); or a concern you must address (59 and below)? Which EQ strategy can you decide to pray about and focus on this month in order to increase your self-management skills?

Social Awareness

The skill of being aware of the emotions of other people, including unspoken cues and the mood in the room, gives you the information you need to manage relationships (TalentSmart®, 2008). Jesus was the master of social awareness. He was the epitome of being in touch with what was going on with other people. He modeled social awareness. He recognized Satan for who he was (Matthew 4) and saw the need for people to be taught (Matthew 5-7). In Matthew 8, Jesus saw and healed the man with leprosy; recognized the faith of the centurion; saw the need for discipleship; and recognized the disciples' fear. In Matthew 9, Jesus appreciated the faith of the friends who helped the paralyzed man; understood the real and spiritual needs (for forgiveness); understood the evil thoughts in hearts; was aware that someone touched His cloak; saw the needs of people; saw that people were harassed and helpless; considered timing; and perceived that people needed shepherding. In Matthew 10, Jesus acknowledged the wolves among the sheep; knew that the disciples needed encouragement (not to worry or be afraid); and understood that the disciples needed to know their value and needed specific instructions. In Matthew 11, Jesus responded to John the Baptist's disciples to meet John's needs; recognized the lack of repentance in multiple towns; and was aware that people were feeling weary and burdened. In Matthew 12, He perceived the hearts of the Pharisees; knew the thoughts of the Pharisees; and understood that the mouth speaks what the heart is full of. In Matthew 13, Jesus showed His social awareness when He used words, parables, and contexts that would make sense to His hearers; understood that some hearts, ears, and eyes were closed and some were blessed; explained Himself; asked questions; and recognized a lack of trust (faith, belief), manifested in hostile indifference.

We can read through the Gospels and note countless additional instances of Jesus' exemplary social awareness. That is a great Bible study for any of the four EQ skills. Jesus was present. He connected with individuals. Jesus showed empathy, which is the capacity to feel another person's feelings, thoughts, or attitudes. He understood the culture in which He lived. Jesus saw people. As the ultimate model of social awareness, He exemplifies the 17 social awareness strategies listed in

Emotional Intelligence 2.0. In Chapter 8, there are scriptures for each of the 17 social-awareness strategies to guide us on HOW to practically improve our self-awareness skills.

Reflection:

Are you able to see/understand people? Are you able to see people as Jesus did? Do you have the empathy to see those around you?

_____

_____

_____

Are you aware of the fact that people are "harassed and helpless, like sheep without a shepherd" (Matthew 9:36)? Do you see the spiritual war Satan is waging here on earth (1 Peter 5:8)?

_____

_____

_____

Is your awareness and reverence for God strong enough to motivate you to try to persuade others (2 Corinthians 5:11)?

_____

_____

_____

Relationship Management

Proverbs 20:5, 1 Corinthians 13:4–8, and Galatians 5:22–23 (discussed in detail at the beginning of this chapter) all describe the skills and characteristics of excellent relationship management. Once again, Jesus is our model of building, strengthening, and deepening connections with people. He was amazing in His ability to manage interactions with others constructively and to a positive outcome. Who else has been as well known for as long as our Lord Jesus Christ? The relationships He built have carried His name to our time (Matthew 28:18–20). He came to earth so that we could have a relationship with God for eternity. He accomplished His mission—the greatest positive outcome. Now it's up to us to carry on and fulfill the Great Commission. With greater spirituality and EQ skills, we can do just that! Jesus exemplifies the relationship management strategies listed in Emotional Intelligence 2.0. In Chapter 8, there are scriptures for each of the 17 relationship management strategies to guide us on HOW to practically improve our self-awareness skills.

Reflection:

What three primary results are you committed to producing with regard to God's will for your emotional intelligence skill levels (include completion date):

_____

_____

_____

_____

_____

_____

Which scriptures can you meditate on to support the results you seek?

_____

_____

_____

_____

_____

_____

Chapter Eight

Build Your EQ Skills – The Bible on *Emotional Intelligence 2.0* Strategies

Though we can change our internal representations (at the subconscious level) in just a few minutes with Time Line Therapy® (Chapter 9), habits also need to be installed and reinforced. We need repentance (Romans 2:4). We need to take radical action to build on any new neural networks we have formed. It takes work to build better skills of self-awareness, self-control, social awareness, and relationship management. The level of our motivation to glorify God in this area will determine the level of our progress. In *Emotional Intelligence 2.0* (2009), Drs. Travis Bradberry and Jean Greaves do an amazing job with the provision of an Emotional Intelligence Appraisal®, a thorough explanation of how to employ our intelligence in a beneficial way, and direction on developing an action plan for increasing EQ. The TalentSmart® workshop on Mastering Self-Awareness, Self-Management, Social Awareness, and Relationship Management is unparalleled.

Emotional Intelligence 2.0 provides 66 strategies for increasing the four core skills of EQ. I obtained TalentSmart® training so I could conduct EQ workshops, and I believe that for many, mastering EQ is the missing link in our ability to reach the spiritual maturity God desires for us. Neither education, experience, knowledge, dedication to spiritual disciplines, nor intellectual acumen serve as adequate predictors of success without considering EQ. Of course, we know that our spirituality and the health of our relationship with God incorporates our daily Bible study, prayer, and fellowship. The effectiveness of each of these depends on our level of emotional maturity. The 66 skill development strategies in *Emotional Intelligence 2.0* provide an answer to HOW we can become more spiritually mature and emotionally intelligent. The strategies can be considered a roadmap to our desired outcome.

As encouraged in Chapter 1, you have taken the appraisal and reflected upon the results (if not, take the test—assessment is imperative!). You know your EQ areas of strength and your EQ areas in need of focus. You have also decided which EQ strategy you will focus on this month and over the next three months. After conducting several of the Mastering EQ workshops, I realized that we, as Christians, would benefit from a resource of biblical principles and examples that correspond to each of the 66 EQ strategies. This Bible companion will be most beneficial after one has taken the EQ Appraisal® and read the information on the strategy selected for the month.

We have a daily, hourly, and minute-by-minute choice of what we will do with our emotions. The 66 strategies help us to optimize our EQ functioning. The related scriptures in this chapter bring the biblical worldview to the science that can powerfully transform our lives! I could comment on every single one of these strategies and could personally select a number of them to focus on for today alone. The Mastering EQ workshop encourages participants to **select one strategy** per month based on the area most in need of attention. For myself and my own sanity, I am eternally grateful that we are covered by the blood of Jesus (Acts 20:28; Romans 3:24–25, 5:9; Colossians 1:20; Ephesians 1:7; Hebrews 9:14; 1 John 1:7; 1 Peter 1:18–19; Revelation 12:11). A quick review of these strategies reminds me (and hopefully all of us) that we have many ways that we can be more like Jesus. And amen that EQ strategies help us to not be overwhelmed with such a goal and task!

Connecting scriptures to these amazing EQ strategies could be a book in itself. Yet, for an initial dive into increasing our EQ skills, I feel that it is imperative to include this section in this book. We pretty much know what we should do as we strive to walk with God. It's great to have transformative resources that give practical recommendations on HOW to do what we want to do with and for God! We can be all the more what God has called us to be. There are many helpful resources outside of God's word, yet the power of His word adds priceless and eternal value to our endeavors to glorify Him. There is no way to list all the related scriptures and examples for the 66 strategies, but I hope that you find the reflection questions and scriptures included to be a good jumpstart!

The lists of strategies and scriptures below will not be optimally transformative without the completion of the *Emotional Intelligence Appraisal*® and a reading of the meaning of your selected strategy of focus. The appraisal takes only ten minutes to complete, but it provides a wealth of information to support you on your journey of increasing your EQ skills. The video lessons included with your appraisal results are fun and encouraging. The scriptures listed below for the 66 *Emotional Intelligence 2.0* strategies can best be processed through considering the questions as you study each of the corresponding strategies in the Emotional Intelligence 2.0 book. **As you select your EQ strategy for each month, also read the corresponding scriptures below.** Please download the Scripture references and passages for this chapter from my website (www.cresendajones.com). If additional examples and Scripture passages come to mind, feel free to let me know.

Reflection:

1. *What two or three things stand out to you the most in the scriptures (for each strategy)?*

2. *Are the principles in these scriptures evident in your life?*

3. *What new or deepened conviction have you gotten from these scriptures?*

4. *What decision can you make today so that the Scriptures can transform your level of EQ and personal life? What decision today will help you to grow spiritually in your walk with God?*

And if the Spirit of him who raised Jesus from the dead is living in you, he who raised Christ from the dead will also give life to your mortal bodies because of his Spirit who lives in you. (Romans 8:11)

Mastering Self-Awareness Strategies

Bradberry & Greaves (2009) share 15 strategies that will help increase our self-awareness skills, love, and the evidence of God's Holy Spirit in our lives. In *Emotional Intelligence 2.0* there are descriptions of each of the strategies that, with intentional focus, can strengthen our EQ. With Jesus as our perfect example, we can work to master these skills so we can be more like Him. The 15 self-awareness strategies are (p. 63):

1. Quit Treating Your Feelings as Good or Bad
2. Observe the Ripple Effect from Your Emotions
3. Lean into Your Discomfort

4. Feel Your Emotions Physically

5. Know Who and What Pushes Your Buttons

6. Watch Yourself Like a Hawk...

7. Keep a Journal about Your Emotions

8. Don't Be Fooled by a Bad Mood

9. Don't Be Fooled by a Good Mood, Either

10. Stop and Ask Yourself Why You Do the Things You Do

11. Visit Your Values

12. Check Yourself

13. Spot Your Emotions in Books, Movies, and Music

14. Seek Feedback

15. Get to Know Yourself under Stress

Reflection:

Which three of the 15 self-awareness strategies do you feel are consistently evident in your life?

_____

_____

_____

Which three of the 15 self-awareness strategies do you feel need attention in order to increase your EQ and spiritual maturity?

_____

_____

_____

After reading the *Emotional Intelligence 2.0* descriptions of the self-awareness strategies of focus, the following scriptures may help you keep your efforts connected to our ultimate goals of walking with God, walking like Jesus, and helping as many as possible to do the same. For easier Bible study, the referenced Scripture passages (a list of Scripture references and entire verses) for each of the four core EQ skills can be found on www.cresendajones.com and printed out.

1. Quit Treating Your Feelings as Good or Bad

Genesis 1:26–28

Deuteronomy 1:17

Ecclesiastes 3:4

Proverbs 20:5

Psalms 25:16–17, 42:5, 44:9–12, 15,

6:6–7, 55:22, 34:18, 139:13–16,

73:25–26, 38:3–4, 17

Matthew 7:1–2

Luke 6:37

John 7:24

John 14:1

Romans 9:2, 8:23

1 Corinthians 3:16

2 Corinthians 6:8–10

2 Corinthians 10:7

1 Peter 5:7, 10

Revelation 3:16

2. Observe the Ripple Effect from Your Emotions

Job 13:23

Psalm 56:8

Proverbs 27:17, 13:20

Lamentations 3:40

Matthew 5:13–16

Matthew 7:12

Mark 12:31

John 11:33

John 13:34–45

John 15:12

Romans 12:2

1 Corinthians 11:28, 31

1 Corinthians 12:26

1 Corinthians 15:33

2 Corinthians 1:3–4

Galatians 5:9

Galatians 6:7

Ephesians 4:29

Colossians 3:12

1 Peter 2:12, 3:15

1 John 3:16

3. Lean into Your Discomfort

Genesis 4:6–7

1 Samuel 14:6

Isaiah 43:2, 53:3

Psalm 119:71

Ruth 1:16

Ecclesiastes 9:10

Lamentations 3:19–25, 27–33

John 12:27

Romans 5:3–5, 8:35

2 Corinthians 1:3–4

2 Corinthians 4:8–10

2 Corinthians 4:16–17

2 Corinthians 5:10

Galatians 6:2

Colossians 1:24

2 Timothy 1:7

2 Timothy 3:12

Hebrews 2:10

Hebrews 11:8–9

Hebrews 11:17–19

Hebrews 11 Faith hall of fame

James 1:2– 4, 12

1 Peter 1:6–7

1 Peter 2:19–21

1 Peter 3:14, 4:1

1 Peter 4:12–13

1 John 2:6

4. Feel Your Emotions Physically

Psalm 6:7	Proverbs 18:14
Psalm 32:2–4	Proverbs 25:20
Proverbs 3:5–8	Isaiah 13:7
Proverbs 4:4	Matthew 11: 28–29
Proverbs 4:20–22	Mark 7:21–23
Proverbs 14:30	Luke 21:26
Proverbs 15 13	1 Corinthians 3:16
Proverbs 16:4	Romans 9:2
Proverbs 17:22	

5. Know Who and What Pushes Your Buttons

Psalm 119:59	1 Corinthians 10:13
Psalm 147:3	1 Corinthians 11:28, 31
Matthew 7:5	2 Corinthians 4:17
Matthew 26:41	Ephesians 6:10–11
Luke 1:37	Colossians 3:15
Acts 15:36–41	James 4:7
Romans 12:3	

6. Watch Yourself Like a Hawk...

Proverbs 4:23	2 Corinthians 13:5
Lamentations 3:40	1 Timothy 4:16
Romans 12:2–3	Hebrews 12:1
1 Corinthians 11:28, 31	1 Peter 5:8

7. Keep a Journal about Your Emotions

All Psalms	Proverbs 14:8
Psalm 26:2	Proverbs 21:2
Psalm 139:23	Galatians 6:4
Proverbs 4:43	1 Corinthians 16:13

8. Don't Be Fooled by a Bad Mood

Proverbs 20:5	James 1:1
Romans 7:15–24	James 1:2–4
2 Corinthians 4:18	

9. Don't Be Fooled by a Good Mood, Either

Proverbs 20:5   Ecclesiastes 7:18

10. Stop and Ask Yourself Why You Do the Things You Do

Proverbs 14:8   Luke 6:48
Proverbs 20:5   Romans 6:12
Proverbs 21:2   Romans 8:5
Proverbs 26:2   Galatians 6:4
Ezekiel 18:27–28   Hebrews 2:1
Haggai 1:5–7   2 Thessalonians 1:11–12
Mark 14:72   1 Peter 1:13

11. Visit Your Values

Psalm 1:1–6   John 17:3
Psalm 119:105   Romans 12:2
Proverbs 2:2–5   1 Corinthians 7:35
Proverbs 4:25   2 Corinthians 13:5
Proverbs 9:10   Colossians 3:2, 23
Isaiah 26:3   Colossians 2:6–8
Matthew 6:33   Hebrews 12:1–2
Matthew 16:26   2 Timothy 1:5–7
Matthew 23:25   Titus 2:11–12
Matthew 24:12–13   1 John 2:6
Luke 6:48   1 John 3:16
John 13:34–35   1 John 4:19

12. Check Yourself

Proverbs 14:8   Romans 12:2–3
Proverbs 18:2   Galatians 6:4
Proverbs 20:25   1 Timothy 3:9
Luke 18:9–14   1 Timothy 4:16
Luke 15:17–24

13. Spot Your Emotions in Books, Movies, and Music

Proverbs 14:8   1 Corinthians 11:28

14. Seek Feedback

Psalm 1:1–6   Proverbs 4:13

Proverbs 1:1-7

Proverbs 12:15

Proverbs 13:10

Proverbs 15:22

Proverbs 19:20–21

Proverbs 20:18

Proverbs 24:6

Proverbs 27:6

Proverbs 28:26

Proverbs 11:14

Jeremiah 17:9

Matthew 7:12

1 Corinthians 15:33

2 Thessalonians 1:11–12

2 Timothy 3:16–17

James 1:5

James 3:17

1 John 4:1

15. Get to Know Yourself under Stress

Psalm 26:2

Psalm 94:19

Psalm 118:5–6

Psalm 119:143

Proverbs 14:8

Matthew 11:28–30

Luke 6:46–49

Luke 21:34

John 14:27

Romans 12:2–3

2 Corinthians 4:7–9

Galatians 6:1, 4

1 John 2:6

Mastering Self-Management Strategies

Bradberry & Greaves (2009) share 17 strategies that will help increase our self-management skills, love, and the evidence of God's Holy Spirit in our lives. In *Emotional Intelligence 2.0* there are descriptions of each of the strategies that, with intentional focus, can strengthen our EQ. With Jesus as our perfect example, we can work to master these skills so we can be more like Him. The 17 self-management strategies are (p. 100):

1. Breathe Right
2. Create an Emotion vs. Reason List
3. Make Your Goals Public
4. Count to Ten
5. Sleep on It
6. Talk to a Skilled Self-Manager
7. Smile and Laugh More
8. Set Aside Some Time in Your Day for Problem Solving
9. Take Control of Your Self-Talk

10. Visualize Yourself Succeeding

11. Clean Up Your Sleep Hygiene

12. Focus Your Attention on Your Freedoms Rather than Your Limitations

13. Stay Synchronized

14. Speak to Someone Who Is Not Emotionally Invested in Your Problem

15. Learn a Valuable Lesson from Everyone You Encounter

16. Put a Mental Recharge into Your Schedule

17. Accept That Change Is Just Around the Corner

Reflection:

Which three of the 17 self-management strategies do you feel are consistently evident in your life??

_____

_____

_____

Which three of the 17 self-management strategies do you feel need attention in order to increase your EQ and spiritual maturity?

_____

_____

_____

After reading the *Emotional Intelligence 2.0* descriptions of the self-management strategies of focus, the following scriptures may help you keep your efforts connected to our ultimate goals of walking with God, walking like Jesus, and helping as many as possible to do the same. For easier Bible study, the referenced scripture passages (a list of Scriptures references and entire verses) for each of the four core EQ skills can be found on www.cresendajones.com and printed out.

1. Breathe Right

1 Corinthians 6:19–20   1 Timothy 4:8

1 Corinthians 14:32
Galatians 5:22–23

2 Timothy 1:7
3 John 1:2

2. Create an Emotion vs. Reason List

Proverbs 12:16
Proverbs 16:32
1 Corinthians 10:13
Galatians 5:16–24

Ephesians 4:1–32
Ephesians 4:26–27
1 Peter 4:7
2 Peter 1:5–9

3. Make Your Goals Public

2 Chronicles 15:7
Ruth 1:16
Proverbs 16:3
Proverbs 21:5
Proverbs 27:17

Ecclesiastes 4:12
Luke 14:28
2 Thessalonians 1:11–12
Philippians 3:13–14

4. Count to Ten

Psalm 139
Proverbs 3:4–6
Proverbs 15:18
Proverbs 18:7
Proverbs 25:28

Proverbs 29:11
Romans 12:21
Galatians 5:22–23
Philippians 4:7
James 1:19

5. Sleep on It

Genesis 29:20
1 Samuel 13:8–14
Proverbs 29:20
Romans 12:12
1 Corinthians 13:4

Galatians 5:16-24
Ephesians 4:2
Philippians 4:6
2 Timothy 1:7
1 Peter 4:7

6. Talk to a Skilled Self-Manager

Matthew 16:24
John 13:15
1 Corinthians 4:16
1 Corinthians 11:1
Ephesians 5:1
Philippians 3:17
Philippians 4:9

1 Thessalonians 1:6
2 Thessalonians 3:7, 9
Hebrews 6:12
1 Peter 1:16
2 Peter 1:5–9
3 John 1:11

7. Smile and Laugh More

Psalm 126:3

Proverbs 15:13–15

Proverbs 15:30

Proverbs 17:22

Proverbs 31:25

Matthew 5:12

Romans 5:3–4

Romans 12:2

8. Set Aside Some Time in Your Day for Problem Solving

Psalm 143:8

Proverbs 3:5–6

Proverbs 6:6–8

Proverbs 14:15

Proverbs 15:22

Proverbs 16:3, 9

Proverbs 19:21

Proverbs 21:5

Luke 14:28–32

Romans 12:2

2 Thessalonians 1:11–12

1 Peter 4:7

2 Peter 1:5–9

9. Take Control of Your Self-Talk

1 Samuel 30:6

Psalm 42:5

Psalm 103:1–22

Proverbs 23:7

Proverbs 25:28

Romans 12:2

2 Corinthians 10:5

Philippians 4:8

Colossians 3:2

Galatians 5:16–24

2 Timothy 1:7

1 Peter 4:7

1 John 2:6

10. Visualize Yourself Succeeding

Genesis 15:5–6

Joshua 1:8

Psalm 23 (images)

Luke 14:28

Matthew 13:34

2 Corinthians 4:18

2 Corinthians 5:7

Philippians 4:7

1 Timothy 3:2

11. Clean Up Your Sleep Hygiene

Psalm 4:8

Psalm 23:1–2

Psalm 46:10

Psalm 91:1–5

Psalm 127:2

Proverbs 3:24

John 14:27

Matthew 8:24

Matthew 11:28–30

12. Focus Your Attention on Your Freedoms Rather than Your Limitations

Psalm 1:1–6

Psalm 118:5

Psalm 119:45

Proverbs 2:2–5

Proverbs 4:25

Isaiah 26:3

Matthew 6:33

Matthew 15:11

John 8:36

Acts 13:38–39

Romans 8:5

Romans 12:2

1 Corinthians 10:13

2 Corinthians 3:17

Galatians 5:1

Galatians 5:13–14, 16–24

Ephesians 3:12

Philippians 4:8

Colossians 3:2

Titus 2:1–8, 11–14

Hebrews 12:1–2

13. Stay Synchronized

Job 27:6

Acts 23:1

Acts 24:16

Romans 2:14–15

Romans 9:1

1 Timothy 1:19

1 Timothy 3:2

2 Timothy 1:3

Titus 1:8

1 Peter 3:16

1 John 3:21

14. Speak to Someone Who Is Not Emotionally Invested in Your Problem

1 Kings 12:6–7

Proverbs 1:7

Proverbs 3:5–6

Proverbs 11:14

Proverbs 12:15

Proverbs 19:20

Proverbs 24:6

Proverbs 28:26

Ecclesiastes 4:9–13

James 1:5

15. Learn a Valuable Lesson from Everyone You Encounter

Proverbs 1:5

Proverbs 1:7

Proverbs 3:11–12

Proverbs 9:9

Proverbs 10:17

Proverbs 12:1

Proverbs 18:15

1 Corinthians 4:6–16

Philippians 3:17

Philippians 4:9

Colossians 2:8

Colossians 3:16

1 Thessalonians 5:11

2 Timothy 2:2

Proverbs 25:4   2 Thessalonians 3:7–9
Matthew 28:18–20

16. Put a Mental Recharge into Your Schedule

Genesis 2:2–3   Mark 6:31–32
Exodus 23:12   John 16:31
Exodus 33:14   Romans 12:1
1 Samuel 40:31   1 Corinthians 6:19–20
Psalm 4:8   1 Corinthians 9:26–27
Psalm 23   1 Corinthians 10:31
Psalm 37:7   Philippians 4:6–7
Psalm 127:2   1 Timothy 4:8
Proverbs 31:17   1 Peter 4:7
Isaiah 26:3   1 John 2:6
Matthew 11:28–30

17. Accept That Change Is Just around the Corner

Psalm 119:50   Luke 12:47
Proverbs 6:6–8   Luke 21:36
Proverbs 16:1–33   Romans 8:28
Proverbs 22:3   1 Corinthians 2:9
Ezekiel 38:7   1 Corinthians 9:22
Matthew 24:13   2 Corinthians 9:8
Matthew 24:44   Ephesians 4:1–32; 11–16
Matthew 25:1–46   1 Peter 1:13

Mastering Social Awareness Strategies

Bradberry & Greaves (2009) share 17 strategies that will help increase our social awareness skills, love, and the evidence of God's Holy Spirit in our lives. In *Emotional Intelligence 2.0* there are descriptions of each of the strategies that, with intentional focus, can strengthen our EQ. With Jesus as our perfect example, we can work to master these skills so we can be more like Him. The 17 social awareness strategies are (p. 138):

1. Greet People by Name
2. Watch Body Language
3. Make Timing Everything
4. Develop a Back-Pocket Question

5. Don't Take Notes at Meetings

6. Plan Ahead for Social Gatherings

7. Clear Away the Clutter

8. Live in the Moment

9. Go on a 15-Minute Tour

10. Watch EQ at the Movies

11. Practice the Art of Listening

12. Go People Watching

13. Understand the Rules of the Culture Game

14. Test for Accuracy

15. Step into Their Shoes

16. Seek the Whole Picture

17. Catch the Mood of the Room

Reflection:

Which three of the 17 social awareness strategies do you feel are consistently evident in your life?

_____

_____

_____

Which three of the 17 social awareness strategies do you feel need attention in order to increase your EQ and spiritual maturity?

_____

_____

_____

After reading the *Emotional Intelligence 2.0* descriptions of the social awareness strategies of focus, the following scriptures may help you keep your efforts connected to our ultimate goals of walking with God, walking like Jesus, and helping as many as possible to do the same. For easier Bible study, the referenced scripture passages (a list of Scripture references and entire verses) for each of the four core EQ skills can be found on www.cresendajones.com and printed out.

1. Greet People by Name

Matthew 7:12

Matthew 19:19

Matthew 22:39

Matthew 25:40

Luke 1:37

Luke 6:31

John 15:12

John 13:34–35

Romans 12:10

Galatians 5:14

Philippians 2:4

Hebrews 13:2

1 Peter 5:5

2. Watch Body Language

Psalm 38:10

Proverbs 2:2

Proverbs 12:25

Proverbs 15:30

Proverbs 16:30–32

Isaiah 50:4–7

Matthew 6:22–23

Luke 11:34

3. Make Timing Everything

Psalm 46:10

Ecclesiastes 3

Ecclesiastes 8:5–6

Jeremiah 8:7

Mark 8:17–18

John 7:6

Romans 8:28

Galatians 6:3

Philippians 2:4

2 Timothy 4:2

Hebrews 13:16

4. Develop a Back-Pocket Question

Proverbs 17:17

Luke 6:31

John 15:12–13

Romans 12:10, 16

1 Corinthians 13:4–8

Ephesians 4:32

Hebrews 10:24

1 John 4:7, 11

5. Don't Take Notes at Meetings

1 Samuel 16:7

2 Chronicles 16:9a

Job 34:21

Psalm 32:8

Proverbs 15:3

Proverbs 16:2b

Proverbs 20:12

2 Corinthians 4:18

6. Plan Ahead for Social Gatherings

Proverbs 14:15–16

Proverbs 21:5

Acts 17:23

Ephesians 5:15–17

1 Peter 5:2

7. Clear Away the Clutter

Proverbs 18:2

Proverbs 18:13

Philippians 2:3–4

Titus 3:2

James 1:19

8. Live in the Moment

Matthew 6:34

Mark 5:24–34 (Jesus' example)

Luke 19:1–9 (Jesus' example)

9. Go on a 15-minute Tour

Genesis 4:6

Exodus 18:14

1 Samuel 17:22–26

Proverbs 20:5

Luke 24:17

Acts 17:23

10. Watch EQ at the Movies

See # 9 above - Go on a 15-minute Tour

11. Practice the Art of Listening

Proverbs 18:2

Proverbs 18:13

Ephesians 5:1–2

James 1:19

1 Peter 5:2

12. Go People Watching

See # 9 above - Go on a 15-minute Tour

13. Understand the Rules of the Culture Game

Genesis 3:9, 11, 13

Matthew 12:46–50

Luke 5:17–26

John 8:1–11

1 John 2:6

14. Test for Accuracy

Genesis 3:9, 11, 13

Proverbs 20:5

Matthew 12:46–50

Luke 5:17–26

John 8:1–11

Romans 12:2

I John 4:1

15. Step into Their Shoes

Psalm 103:13–14   John 11:33, 35
Psalm 139:1–3   Romans 12:15
Matthew 7:12   Galatians 6:2
Matthew 9:36   Ephesians 5:1
Matthew 14:14   Philippians 2:4
Matthew 22:39   1 John 2:6

16. Seek the Whole Picture

Proverbs 3:5   Lamentations 3:40
Proverbs 15:22   Romans 12:3
Proverbs 16:25   Galatians 6:3–5
Jeremiah 17:9   Ephesians 5:1–2

17. Catch the Mood of the Room

Matthew 9:36   John 11:35
John 6:15   Acts 17:23

Mastering Relationship Management Strategies

Bradberry & Greaves (2009) share 17 strategies that will help increase our relationship management skills, love, and the evidence of God's Holy Spirit in our lives. In *Emotional Intelligence 2.0* there are descriptions of each of the strategies that, with intentional focus, can strengthen our EQ. With Jesus as our perfect example, we can work to master these skills so we can be more like Him. The 17 relationship management strategies are (p. 179):

1. Be Open and Be Curious
2. Enhance Your Natural Communication Style
3. Avoid Giving Mixed Signals
4. Remember the Little Things That Pack a Punch
5. Take Feedback Well
6. Build Trust
7. Have an "Open-Door" Policy
8. Only Get Mad on Purpose
9. Don't Avoid the Inevitable

10. Acknowledge the Other Person's Feelings

11. Complement the Person's Emotions or Situation

12. When You Care, Show It

13. Explain Your Decisions, Don't Just Make Them

14. Make Your Feedback Direct and Constructive

15. Align Your Intention with Your Impact

16. Offer a "Fix-It" Statement during a Broken Conversation

17. Tackle a Tough Conversation

Reflection:

Which three of the 17 relationship management strategies do you feel are consistently evident in your life?

_____

_____

_____

Which three of the 17 relationship management strategies do you feel need attention in order to increase your EQ and spiritual maturity?

_____

_____

_____

After reading the *Emotional Intelligence 2.0* descriptions of the relationship management strategies of focus, the following scriptures may help you keep your efforts connected to our ultimate goals of walking with God, walking like Jesus, and helping as many as possible to do the same. For easier Bible study, the referenced scripture passages (a list of Scripture references and entire verses) for each of the four core EQ skills can be found on www.cresendajones.com and printed out.

1. Be Open and Be Curious

Proverbs 13:20

Proverbs 20:5

Mark 12:29–31

John 13:34–35

Galatians 6:2

Ephesians 5:21

James 1:2–4

James 5:16

2 Corinthians 6:11–13

2 Corinthians 12:9–12

1 John 1:7

2. Enhance Your Natural Communication Style

1 Corinthians 13

Ephesians 4:2–3, 29

Colossians 3:23

3. Avoid Giving Mixed Signals

Matthew 18:15–17

Luke 6:31

John 8:32

Ephesians 4:2–4

Philippians 2:5

Colossians 3:23

4. Remember the Little Things That Pack a Punch

Luke 6:31

Romans 12:10

Romans 13:8

Ephesians 5:1–2

Philippians 2:3

Colossians 3:23

1 Peter 5:2

5. Take Feedback Well

Proverbs 11:12

Proverbs 13:20

Proverbs 27:6a

Isaiah 5:21

Ephesians 4:2–3

Ephesians 5:21

Philippians 2:3–7

1 Peter 3:8

1 Peter 5:6–7

6. Build Trust

Proverbs 16:16

Proverbs 18:24

Romans 12:10

Romans 14:13

John 15:13

1 Corinthians 13:1-8

Galatians 5:13

Ephesians 4:2–3

Ephesians 4:29

Ephesians 5:1–2

Philippians 4:10

1 Peter 4:8

1 Peter 5:2

7. Have an "Open-Door" Policy

Mark 12:29–31

1 Corinthians 13

Ephesians 5:21

1 John 2:6

8. Only Get Mad on Purpose

1 Corinthians 13:4–8

Philippians 2:5

2 Timothy 1:7

1 Peter 4:8

1 John 2:6

Ephesians 4:26

9. Don't Avoid the Inevitable

Proverbs 17:17

Proverb 27:6a

Matthew 18:15–17

John 14:27

10. Acknowledge the Other Person's Feelings

Luke 6:31

Romans 12:10

1 Corinthians 13

1 Peter 3:8

1 Peter 5:2

11. Complement the Person's Emotions or Situation

Philippians 2:3

Philippians 4:8

1 Thessalonians 5:11

Hebrews 3:13

Hebrews 10:24–25

12. When You Care, Show It

Proverbs 11:25, 17

Proverbs 18:24

Matthew 22:39

Luke 6:38

John 3:16a

John 13:14

John 13:34–35

John 15:13

Acts 20:35

Romans 12:10

Romans 13:8

Galatians 5:13

Ephesians 5:1–2

Philippians 2:5

Hebrews 10:24–25

1 Peter 3:8

1 Peter 4:8

1 John 2:6

13. Explain Your Decisions, Don't Just Make Them

Genesis 2:18

Luke 6:31

Romans 12:16

1 Corinthians 13

Ephesians 5:21

Philippians 2:3

Hebrews 10:24–25

2 Timothy 1:7

1 Peter 5:2

14. Make Your Feedback Direct and Constructive

Proverbs 27:6a
Matthew 18:15–17
Mark 12:29–31

Romans 15:14
Ephesians 4:29
1 Peter 4:8

15. Align Your Intention with Your Impact

Mark 12:29–31
John 13:34–35
Romans 12:10
Romans 13:8
1 Corinthians 13

Colossians 3:21
Hebrews 10:24–25
2 Thessalonians 1:11–12
2 Timothy 1:7
1 John 2:6

16. Offer a "Fix-It" Statement during a Broken Conversation

Matthew 18:15–17
Luke 6:31
John 14:27
1 Corinthians 1:10

1 Corinthians 13
Ephesians 5:21
Philippians 2:3
1 Peter 5:6

17. Tackle a Tough Conversation

Proverbs 27:6a
Matthew 18:15–17
John 14:27
1 Corinthians 11:28, 31
1 Corinthians 13
2 Corinthians 13:5
Philippians 2:5
2 Timothy 1:7
Hebrews 10:24–25

1 Peter 3:8
1 Peter 5:6–7
1 Peter 4:8
1 Timothy 4:16
Hebrews 12:1
1 Peter 5:6-8

Chapter Nine

Time Line Therapy® – Transforming Our Neurology

Be made new in the attitude of your minds.
—Ephesians 4:23

Our thoughts are mainly controlled by our subconscious,... and you cannot change the subconscious mind by just thinking about it.... The subconscious mind is like a tape player. Until you change the tape, it will not change.
—Bruce H. Lipton, Ph.D.

A memory without the emotional charge is called wisdom.
—Dr. Joe Dispenza

How do we eliminate longstanding emotional baggage? How do we purge the toxic emotional residue (left over from emotions such as anger, sadness, fear, hurt, guilt, and shame) that regularly plagues our hearts? How do we eradicate the negative beliefs that we consistently ruminate on? The good news is that we can transform our neurology.

Yet the reality for many of us is that we have frequently thought, felt, or heard from others the statements in the list below. Please note how often you have thought or felt the statements **in the course of the last month.** Place your response in the blank column on the right in the table below.

Survey scale: 1 – Never, 2 – Rarely, 3 – Sometimes, 4 – Very Often, 5 – Always

1.		I am not enough.
2.		I have to be "perfect" to be accepted (and/or) to stay out of trouble.
3.		Others seem to be okay when they make mistakes, but I have to do everything right.
4.		No matter what I do, things won't change.
5.		It is not safe to have emotions or to be vulnerable.
6.		When I repress my emotions, no one "gets hurt."
7.		I am an addict or I have an addictive personality.
8.		I am powerless.
9.		I will never actually change/I cannot change.
10.		I do not think I deserve to be taken care of or loved. I am unworthy of devotion, dedication, loyalty, sacrifice, attention, energy.
11.		It is because of me that my parents have problems, fights, are separated/divorced.
12.		I brought this sexual assault on myself or I deserved to be sexually assaulted.
13.		I do not want others to feel that I am a mess or to worry about me.
14.		I have no or little value without having a significant partner. I can't handle being alone.
15.		I cannot focus.
16.		I cannot control my anxiety.
17.		I am depressed.
18.		I cannot handle anything else. I can't handle this. I can't do this.
19.		It does not matter if I'm alive.
20.		I have to deal with this on my own. No one cares.
21.		I cannot get motivated.
22.		I am too much. People can't deal with me. I am a problem. I am intolerable.
23.		I am only valued when I am giving. I always have to give more than I receive because I need to be valued.
24.		I should not have any needs or I am not allowed to have or express needs. I feel "needy" when I express my personal needs.
25.		My needs are not important, not a priority.
26.		I cannot trust people or the world around me.
27.		I cannot do this anymore; I'm done with this child.
28.		It is difficult to love me.
29.		I need to be invisible to be "okay" or for things to be "okay." I wish I were invisible. I feel invisible.
30.		Anger protects me.
31.		I have to protect myself at all times (be hypervigilant).
		TOTAL SCORE

If you, or someone you love, have thought item number 18 or have had any suicidal or homicidal thoughts, please contact a mental health professional right now. In the United States, the **National Suicide Hotline is available at 1-800-273-8255.**

The more 4s and 5s you have, the more Time Line Therapy® can help you transform your internal representations and neurology. I have personally read countless books, stayed committed to spiritual transformation efforts, worked with licensed therapists since 2000, had steady discipling mentors, and consistently worked with great effort to get beyond the dysfunctional thinking, emotions, and patterns of relating that seemed to have become a part of my DNA. Researchers are finding that stress even impacts our gene expression (Van Der Kolk, 2014). I experienced firsthand the immense impact of stress when repressed memories and emotions came back to me during my early college years.

After extensive learning in a Bible study series, I was baptized during my first year of college at the University of North Carolina at Charlotte. Our church later went through what we called a "reconstruction" process during which we all were called to recommit to God's standard of discipleship and commitment. A traumatic incident resurfaced at this time. I vividly remember that during my "reconstruction meeting," I discussed a sexual trauma that I experienced at the age of 12. I believe that I had possibly mentioned this event during my original Bible studies in 1985. As I shared about this incident of being sexually assaulted when I was 12 years old by a 19-year-old man in our neighborhood, I cried in such a way that it seemed as though I had not ever discussed that event. At the time the incident happened (the summer of 1979), I did not even talk to my mom or any other key people in my life about it. For some reason, the unbelievable weight of this inappropriate and unwarranted shame kept me silent. I do not recall thinking that what the 19-year-old man did was my fault. Yet, for some reason, I kept the incident suppressed as much as I possibly could. I am sure that I was in shock and did not want to let anyone know what had happened. Yet during the reconstruction conversation, as I discussed this traumatic incident, my skin broke out in visible hives (on my arms). Sadly, I don't recall any of the folks in the meeting suggesting that I see a professional therapist. I imagine that they did not know what to do except to attempt to comfort me and point me to God's desire to forgive everyone—including the 19-year-old offender.

It is true that God wants us to forgive others. **And it is also true**

that forgiveness involves a process that includes acknowledging our thoughts and feelings. Joseph's story with his brothers and how he wept bitterly before the meeting in which he extended forgiveness (Genesis 43:30) is a great example. I do thank God that I have now had the opportunity to work through the shame and trauma of what I experienced. I have also been blessed to use Time Line Therapy® to eliminate the destructive emotional residue connected to that event and therefore have released it fully, which includes forgiveness.

When I look back at how the negative impact of the assault once permeated every aspect of my life, I am saddened that our society seemed to lack a clear direction on the need to refer individuals who have experienced trauma to mental health professionals. In my own life, I was subconsciously carrying all the damaging emotional residue related to this sexual assault. I also realized that I had no idea how to handle or effectively process other significant emotional events such as the grief related to my parents' separation and divorce. And I did not have the resources nor EQ skills to effectively deal with the damage and brokenness that came from living with my stepfather, who had a drinking problem.

At some point I realized that even with years of professional therapy and rigorous spiritual and emotional work, I was not able to loose the claws of the emotions in my heart, mind, and soul. Those emotions seemed like a ball and chain as they impacted my personal and professional relationships. In 2012, I was diagnosed with smoldering myeloma, lupus, and fibromyalgia. Prior to that, I had taken medication for anxiety and depression. In 2013, I had to medically retire from a career in education administration. A few years after submitting the application, I received Social Security disability. Anyone familiar with that United States Federal Government system and process knows that it seems like you have to be half dead to be approved for those benefits. I was totally feeling depressed after my rheumatologist had tried a couple of prescription medications to no avail. As I proceeded on this medical journey, my oncologist did not approve the use of the last rheumatology prescription option. He noted that this medication would need to be reserved for use in the event that the smoldering myeloma progressed to multiple myeloma.

After retiring, I began working toward a professional counseling degree to keep my brain busy. Though I had already completed a Life Coach Certification program, I signed up for a Neuro Strategic Coaching Certificate program. It was during this intensive training that my supervisor introduced the class to Time Line Therapy® and a parts integration technique. At the time, I felt that I was in survival mode and just trying to make it through all the physical challenges that came with feeling depressed and anxious about lupus, smoldering myeloma, and the lack of helpful medical treatments. I am typically up for trying anything that would help me or move me forward, so when my supervisor asked for a volunteer to demonstrate the power of the parts integration therapeutic technique, I jumped at the opportunity. It was my understanding that in participating in the parts integration technique, I could eliminate a limiting belief. I was aware that I had been holding on to the limiting belief that I "just was not good enough," even though I intellectually knew better. I had long ago adopted this limiting belief during the many challenging events and circumstances in my childhood. My environment back then did not foster the development of EQ, safety, self-esteem, or the peace that God offers.

After volunteering for the demonstration of parts integration and seeing instant results, I wondered what had actually happened—when, where, why, and how? I was amazed by my classmates saying that it looked like I had had a facelift! The heavy weight of the limiting belief was lifted. It no longer made sense. I wanted to understand how to keep the limiting belief that "I am not good enough" out of my head, mental tapes, and heart. This limiting belief had dogged me and all my transformation efforts my entire life. Thus, after years of research and exhausting all my known options, I jumped on the opportunity to learn about the possibility of optimal health with the Tad James Co. Time Line Therapy® breakthrough program. The hope that there were more possibilities out there was motivating!

I also signed up for the NLP Coaching and Time Line Therapy® Practitioner level training. Although I lacked sufficient funds for such a course, God provided a way. Once I found out that master practitioner level training addressed medical issues, I enrolled in that course too.

Transforming Our Neurology with Time Line Therapy®

As discussed in Chapter 4, our unconscious mind is where our emotions and memories are stored. Our unconscious mind also controls and maintains all perceptions. It maintains instincts and generates habits. Thus, if we desire effectual, powerful, and the most efficient transformation of our hearts, minds, and souls, change must take place at the unconscious level. As we discussed with the brain wave information, learnings are best retained when we access our unconscious minds. We can rewire our neural circuits most efficiently and effectively when we work toward change by accessing our subconscious mind. **In order to master our mind, we must work with the power of the unconscious mind.**

When we experience something negative, traumatic, or emotionally painful, the emotions and thoughts remain in our nervous system and affect our current state (mental, emotional, and physical) and experiences. The anger, sadness, fear, hurt, guilt, grief, frustration, shame, anxiety, and stress build up in our neurology. "A person's Time Line represents their mental photo album" (GoodTherapy, 2015). "The internal programming is often the mechanism that is responsible for our outward expressions of emotions" (GoodTherapy, 2015). The Time Line Therapy® process provides freedom from past negative thoughts and emotional residue that should no longer be carried with us. The process allows one to release the toxic emotional sewage and let go of limiting decisions or beliefs connected to past events.

Time Line Therapy® allows us to let go of thoughts such as "I'm not good enough," "There is something wrong with me," "I am a failure," and "I am powerless." These negatively charged emotions and limiting beliefs or decisions are replaced by positive learnings and resources for ourselves and our future. Along with eliminating the negative emotional baggage, **the process changes our physiology and state of mind instantaneously** (Figure 3.1). After completing the Time Line Therapy® breakthrough process, one "can react to present experiences based on present conditions and not react to situations that present themselves today based on emotions linked to previous life events" (GoodTherapy, 2015). In addition, Time Line Therapy® also allows us to design our future as we wish as opposed to our lives being driven by inappropriate emotions and internal representations. With the emotional baggage and unconscious tapes eliminated, we can envision and realize the "life to the full" (John 10:10) that God has planned!

I experienced and was trained to provide the breakthrough process by Tad James Co., the creator of Time Line Therapy®. These techniques allow us to work to release the effects of past negative experiences and change unhealthy neuro-programming in just minutes. In all my years of receiving professional support from multiple licensed therapists, books, and programs, I have never seen anything as effective and efficient. The possibilities, after releasing the harmful emotional residue, are endless. We can take hold of love, joy, peace, patience, kindness, goodness, faithfulness, gentleness, and self-control (Galatians 5:22)! We can love God, ourselves, and others as 1 Corinthians 13 prescribes. We do not have to be controlled by emotions that escalate into inappropriate and unwarranted baggage.

The Transformational Time Line Therapy® breakthrough process includes:

1. Taking a Detailed Personal History to discover the root cause of problems

2. Establishment of goals and desired outcomes

3. Time Line Therapy® techniques supported by Neuro Linguistic Programming – the elimination of negative emotional baggage and limiting decisions and beliefs connected to past events

4. Individualized tasks

5. A 30-day follow up call

I encourage you to really take in what you just read. Can you imagine eliminating all the negative emotional sewage connected to the significant events in your life? Can you imagine the result of this change in your internal representations? Can you imagine the result of this process on your emotions and personality? Can you fathom the clarity, peace, and freedom that is possible once all the emotional baggage and limiting beliefs connected to past events are finally eliminated? Can you imagine the additional emotional and mental capacity of your mind without the negative emotional residue and limiting beliefs that have been with you since as far back as you can recall? Yes, step three of the Time Line Therapy® process really does eliminate negatively charged emotions and limiting beliefs connected to past events.

Once a person has completed the Time Line Therapy® breakthrough process, they can still remember past events, yet they do so with an absence of the negative charge of the old emotions. There is also a "future pacing" during which the person realizes they cannot find unwarranted or inappropriate emotions in their future. I feel in awe each time I facilitate this Time Line Therapy® breakthrough process! I get to see amazing miracles with each client who has decided that it is time to forget the past and strain toward what is ahead (Philippians 3:13). I always wanted to get rid of the emotional baggage I was carrying, but I just didn't know HOW. As a disciple committed to the Bible as my standard, I always talked about whatever was bothering me, but I just could not seem to resolve the emotions connected to whatever had happened. The power of the negative emotional sewage was still with me and was fueling ungodly thoughts and behaviors. I am immensely grateful that God allowed me to be exposed to this powerful Time Line Therapy® process that answers my HOW questions!

The Time Line Therapy® breakthrough process does not make us robots or like Mr. Spock on Star Trek. Unless we have had the temporal lobe portion (including the amygdala, hippocampus, hypothalamus, cingulate gyrus, and ventral tegmental area) of our brain removed, it is highly unlikely that we would become an emotionless and detached Vulcan like the science officer and First Officer on the Starship Enterprise. Actually, Mr. Spock told us that *"Change is the essential process of all existence."* **With God and the Time Line Therapy® breakthrough process we can see the Romans 12:2 transformation we desire. God has designed our brain's limbic system, and we can optimize this gift!**

After completing the process of eliminating negative emotional charges and limiting beliefs or decisions from our internal representations, we can face our future with appropriate and warranted emotions as opposed to inappropriate or unwarranted ones. Many success stories (but not all) can be found on my website: www.cresendajones.com. Because of its effectiveness, the breakthrough process using Time Line Therapy® has become my favorite therapeutic modality to help those who feel stuck and those who are not realizing desired goals in their personal, spiritual, and professional lives. We can live as the conquerors God has already decreed (Romans 8:37)! Personally, even if I am not physically feeling 100%, my inner life, emotions, and internal representations have been transformed, so that I can still be powerfully used by God. Our families and world desperately need us all to be at our best. With the renewing of our minds, we can transform ourselves (Romans 12:2) and humankind! We can reject Satan's schemes, change the recordings in our minds (the negative cognitions) and live in line with God's word!

Neuro linguistic programming, which was described in Chapter 4 under "The NLP Model of Communication," is a powerful tool used during Time Line Therapy®. In comparing traditional talk therapy with the Time Line Therapy® transformation process, Tad James Co., LLC (2018) notes:

Counseling/Therapy Typically:	NLP Coaching Typically:
1. Asks WHY?	1. Asks HOW, WHAT & WHAT IF?
2. Avoids undesirable emotions (such as anger, sadness, fear, hurt & guilt)	2. Considers the intention & purpose of emotions
3. Seeks healing of past trauma	3. Focuses on creating a compelling future—getting rid of past obstacles
4. Diagnoses & addresses symptoms	4. Assumes health & desires to create a better future
5. Focuses on content, old pain, trauma	5. Focuses on process by which blocks are created & builds control over inner capabilities
6. Progress is time consuming	6. Changes amaze clients – fast & fun!
7. Therapist/doctor treats	7. A partnership. Coaching to move beyond challenges to wins. Client is responsible to achieve outcomes. Client has control over results.

Although it is true that for some people, basic relaxation techniques are very helpful, Goleman (1995) reports that scientifically, relaxation methods are typically not enough in themselves. Studies Goleman references note that "Worriers" also need to actively challenge their worrisome thoughts. If they do not,

> The worry spiral will keep coming back. So, the next step is to take a critical stance toward their assumptions: Is it very probable that the dreaded event will occur? Is it necessarily the case that there is only one or no alternative to letting it happen? Are there constructive steps to be taken? Does it really help to run through these same anxious thoughts over and over? This combination of mindfulness and healthy skepticism would, presumably, act as a brake on the neural activation that underlies low-grade anxiety. Actively generating such thoughts may prime the circuitry that can inhibit the limbic driving of worry; at the same time, actively inducing a relaxed state counters the signals for anxiety the emotional brain is sending throughout the body (p. 69).

Though not professionally connected, 10 years after the development of Time Line Therapy®, the author of *Emotional Intelligence* describes the process rather well.

In the Time Line Therapy® breakthrough process that accesses our unconscious minds, a client is relaxed and creatively visualizes their life and event time line. To release or eliminate the negative charge of emotions connected to past events, the client considers with what learnings they can replace the damaging emotional charge. Though there is information online, **do not try these** powerful techniques without the required and extensive training (www.nlpcoaching.com).

Following the elimination of negative emotional charges and limiting beliefs and decisions (connected to past events), clients are called to act in the direction of their new learnings, thoughts, and convictions. This approach is in line with Goleman's prescription for tackling worry and anxiety. Just as God speaks of the spirits coming back seven times stronger (Matthew 12:43–45), Goleman notes that we must actively challenge our thoughts. Doing so is akin to "filling our house" so as to uninvite any potential unwelcome guests from filling the space. God calls us to put to death whatever belongs to our earthly nature—our old self (Colossians 3:1–17). He instructs us to set our mind on things above and put on our new self. In the Time Line Therapy® breakthrough process, negative emotional baggage is subconsciously replaced with positive learnings for our future so that we can focus on what we want versus any toxic emotional residue or limiting beliefs or decisions. The best way to predict our future is to create it (Dispenza, n.d.)! With the Time Line Therapy® breakthrough process, we are empowered to change our internal representations, emotional states, and physiology (Figure 3.1). A fellow disciple and Time Line Therapy® practitioner described it best: Time Line Therapy® heals where talk therapy provides coping and managing strategies. I am grateful for healing.

God's Word on Transformation

God is clear on the fact that we are to be transformed. Here are a few English Standard Version scriptures for your study:

- 2 Corinthians 3:18 – And we all, with unveiled face, beholding the glory of the Lord, are being transformed into the same image from one degree of glory to another. For this comes from the Lord who is the Spirit.

- 2 Thessalonians 3:5 – May the Lord direct your hearts to the love of God and to the steadfastness of Christ.

- Acts 3:19 – Repent therefore, and turn back, that your sins may be blotted out, that times of refreshing may come from the presence of the Lord.

- 2 Corinthians 5:17 – Therefore, if anyone is in Christ, he is a new creation. The old has passed away; behold, the new has come.

- Ezekiel 36:26 – And I will give you a new heart, and a new spirit I will put within you. And I will remove the heart of stone from your flesh and give you a heart of flesh.

- Philippians 1:6 – And I am sure of this, that he who began a good work in you will bring it to completion at the day of Jesus Christ.

- Galatians 2:20 – I have been crucified with Christ. It is no longer I who live, but Christ who lives in me. And the life I now live in the flesh I live by faith in the Son of God, who loved me and gave himself for me.

- Psalm 51:10–12 –
  Create in me a clean heart, O God,
  and renew a right spirit within me.
  Cast me not away from your presence,
  and take not your Holy Spirit from me.
  Restore to me the joy of your salvation,
  and uphold me with a willing spirit.

Reflection:

What does God's word inspire you to tackle and transform in your life?

_____

_____

_____

What negative significant emotional events (when you felt angry, sad, fearful, hurt, or guilty) still hold a place in your mind and emotions? With which events is there still a negative emotional charge?

_____

_____

_____

_____

_____

_____

Can you imagine your life without that emotional baggage? What would your life look, sound, and feel like?

_____

_____

_____

_____

_____

_____

_____

_____

What dreams and goals could you accomplish without that emotional baggage?

_____

_____

_____

_____

_____

_____

_____

_____

Does God want you to have "life to the full" (John 10:10)? Can God accomplish anything and everything? What dreams and goals do you feel have been impossible? Are there any limiting beliefs blocking your faith in God's power and keeping you from having healthy self-esteem?

_____

_____

_____

_____

_____

_____

_____

_____

_____

To what extent are you open to tools and processes that can powerfully change your internal representations? Additional information can be found at www. cresendajones.com. I offer a free consult for anyone interested in the Time Line Therapy® breakthrough process.

_____

_____

_____

_____

_____

_____

_____

_____

Chapter Ten

Three Requisites for Mind Changes and Soul Transformations

So repent [change your inner self—your old way of thinking,
regret past sins] and return [to God—seek His purpose for your life],
so that your sins may be wiped away [blotted out, completely erased],
so that times of refreshing may come from the presence of the Lord
[restoring you like a cool wind on a hot day].
—Acts 3:19 (AMP)

"Do you want to get well?"
—Jesus, John 5:6

Scientists and practitioners continue to learn absolutely amazing things about how to help us transform our lives (Romans 12:2). It is exciting and encouraging to see how new developments correlate with and are supported by God's word. As our sister in Christ and author Jeanie Shaw has said, psychology reflects what God already knows. It was not until I was introduced to NLP Coaching and Time Line Therapy® that I heard of the three requisites, or requirements, for change (Tad James Co., 2018). Of course, God had already revealed these principles, but the developers of this revolutionary process have noted the following requirements for transformation in our lives:

1. Getting Rid of Toxic Emotional Residue & Limiting Decisions; Parts Integration, Setting Values & Creating the Future

2. Taking Radical Action (Includes Enforcing Your Boundaries)

3. Focusing on What You Want (Your Evaluations Become Suggestions to the Unconscious Mind)

To win our spiritual battle against the forces of evil, we all know that we must take radical, massive, and relentless action. Regarding the first requisite, we have been clearly instructed on taking captive every thought and making it obedient to Christ (2 Corinthians 10:5). We have to focus on constant and never-ending improvement as we strive to be more and more like Jesus. This is what the second requirement is all about. We are told to focus our thinking on what is noble, right, pure, lovely, admirable, excellent, and praiseworthy (Philippians 4:8). This aptly describes the third requisite for a transformed life.

Keep in mind that, where our energy (mental, emotional, and physical) flows, there we go. Toward the objective of change, I had lived the life of a biblical disciple to the best of my ability, worked extremely and intentionally hard, read countless books, received countless hours of professional therapy, attended workshop after workshop and even obtained my master's degree in professional counseling in order to figure out HOW to continue to grow. The reality, though, was that I still could not shake those internal and subconscious negative tapes, narratives, or limiting beliefs. One of my greatest struggles was always feeling that I was not enough. At times, I even felt the opposite, that I was too much. I am very grateful that my supervisor (during my counseling internship) introduced me to NLP Coaching and Time Line Therapy®. I learned how to sustain my altered state (no longer believing that I am not enough) and to continue my own personal growth. This process revolutionized my thinking and even my health.

Getting Rid of Toxic Emotional Residue & Limiting Decisions; Setting Values & Creating the Future

As previously noted, the NLP Model of Communication (Figure 4.2) and scientific research clearly show that our **internal representations (how one perceives things in their mind),** emotional state, and physiology all impact each other. Regarding the first requisite for change, using Time Line Therapy® techniques, clients are empowered to eliminate the harmful emotional charge and limiting beliefs/decisions connected to past events. It is miraculous every time I see anger, sadness, fear, hurt, and guilt disappear from a client's internal representations and be replaced with positive resources and learnings for their future. Once clients have their "learnings," they connect them with supporting scriptures. Even more amazing is how the limiting beliefs/decisions disappear with the technique. I have neither seen nor experienced such a complete level of emotional freedom with any other spiritual or psychological discipline or technique. The ball and chain of negative emotional residue and limiting beliefs/decisions unconsciously disappears, and clients are left with only having to deal with appropriate and warranted emotions in their future.

The process is so efficient (likened to a year of therapy in eight hours), effective, and invaluable that practitioners (including me) offer a money-back guarantee. Though many therapists have clients consciously consider all the significant events that have happened in their lives (review their "time line"), Time Line Therapy® is different in that it is a technique that subconsciously frees people up to focus on their desired future outcomes and success. As you recall from Chapter 4, our emotions are stored in our unconscious mind. When we access our unconscious mind, we can eliminate the negative emotional charges and beliefs where they are stored. Otherwise, we have not transformed the root issue(s).

Time Line Therapy® powerfully and subconsciously replaces all our toxic emotional residue and the limiting beliefs with learnings that we can use as resources for our future. We ensure that the emotional charges connected to the five major emotions of anger, sadness, fear, hurt, and guilt are eliminated in our internal representations. **Emotions are meant to provide information for us in the present.** We are not designed to hold onto the toxic energy or negative charges of emotions and limiting beliefs connected to past events. Please note as you read through this chapter that I have included an extended list of emotions included in the basic five in acknowledgement that some individuals will be better able to connect with or process certain terms instead of others. Instead of our minds, bodies, and hearts being filled with the negative charges of **anger,** vengefulness, rage, fury, indignation, annoyance, and antagonism, we can replace those with what we desire and with what will benefit us. Instead of anger, one can capitalize on love, joy, peace, kindness (Galatians 5:22), calm, contentment, and good will. Consider the last time you felt angry or annoyed. Imagine that if in that moment, you instead had felt a peaceful and serene emotion and state. How do you think that would have impacted what happened next?

Instead of our minds, bodies, and hearts being filled with **sadness,** grief, unhappiness, sorrow, despair, depression, apathy, and indifference, Time Line Therapy® subconsciously eliminates the old energy of those emotions, which allows clients to choose a different emotional state. One can choose joy, cheer, hope, optimism, comfort, courage, contentment, happiness, health, relief, and satisfaction. Instead of **fear,** worry, anxiety, angst, insecurity, insignificance, worthlessness, being overwhelmed, fright, and terror, after Time Line Therapy®, clients no longer feel those old emotions connected to past events or find them in future events. Using the power of the mind and God's Spirit, clients can choose an emotional state of peace, courage, bravery, faith, confidence, assurance, trust, love, calmness, certainty, ease, joy, security, tranquility, hope, serenity, soundness, steadiness, and composure.

Time Line Therapy® replaces the old feelings of **hurt,** resentment, animosity, bitterness, exasperation, ill will, trauma, agony, distress, harm, woundedness, vexation, offense, pain, and suffering. Subconsciously, one installs happiness, forgiveness, serenity, comfort, healing, grace, good will, kindness, sympathy, empathy, and affection. Lastly, the major toxic emotional residue of **guilt,** shame, disgust, disapproval, judgment, loathing, disappointment, revulsion, aversion, remorse, embarrassment, contempt, regret, iniquitousness, self-condemnation, and self-reproach connected to past events is all eliminated. The unconscious learnings are resources that include the acceptance of forgiveness (for self and others), sympathy, empathy, love, affection, freedom, peace, joy, grace, serenity, calmness, and delight. It is miraculous what God allows our brains (conscious and unconscious) to accomplish! These transformed internal representations impact our emotional states and physiology. The three components of the NLP Communication Model (Figure 4.2) determine and control our behavior.

Have you ever noticed or, like me, experienced making a decision to radically repent and were still left feeling the negative emotional residue connected to the situation? Have you ever decided to forgive someone but could not seem to let go of or release the feelings of hurt? It can be discouraging to believe in God's truths regarding forgiveness and make decisions that please God, yet still be left with the old emotions. You have probably heard the recommendation that we need to make decisions and let our emotions catch up with our actions. Goleman (1995) notes that it is easier to change intellectual beliefs than to change feelings. Our early emotional learnings can trigger behavioral reactions that we later need to battle as sin. These behavioral reactions have been "especially hard to eradicate entirely" (Goleman, 1995, p. 156). Time Line Therapy® intervenes in our unconscious mind, where memories and emotions are stored, to interrupt and change the emotional learning that occurred early in life.

As mentioned in the last chapter, we do not become emotionless robots, but with Time Line Therapy® we eliminate the emotional charge and overwrite the subconscious tapes. We become free from emotional baggage and free to engage more fully in the present emotions. Since

95% of what is going on with us is run by our subconscious mind, that is where change, transformation, and learning must take place also! Time Line Therapy® rewires our neurology. It allows us to be free and clear of emotional baggage and limiting beliefs. With work on the subconscious level, we can truly demolish the strongholds and pretentions of anxiety, depression, anger, hurt, and shame (2 Corinthians 10:5). This process, the first requisite, is the tool that allows us to become masters of our minds! "No human quality is beyond change" (Goleman, 1995, p. 223).

Let's revisit the topic of setting values, looking again at the reflection exercise in Chapter 3, which asked you to consider what and who is important to you. You wrote a list of what you value and then placed the things you listed in order of importance. After setting outcomes, eliminating negative emotional charges and limiting decisions, doing parts integration, and testing to make sure the root issue (greater problem) has disappeared, with the Time Line Therapy® breakthrough process, we re-elicit values to make sure motivation can be sustained. Time Line Therapy® techniques even allow us to change the hierarchy of our values to best support our transformation. For instance, a couple of clients did not have God as most important in their lives and values, but they wanted to experience the blessings, peace, transformation, courage, and promises that come with a biblical relationship with God. Thus, we have a procedure that allows us to subconsciously change our values hierarchy so that change can be sustained. We also check ecology to make sure that there are no conflicts or reasons why the client's transformation would be disrupted.

The Tad James Time Line Therapy® breakthrough process also calls us to visualize and consequently "create our future." 1 Peter 1:13 tells us to prepare our minds for action (ESV) and that our minds must be clear and ready for action (GW). To support this change requisite, clients are taken through a technique by which a specific goal is inserted, at the unconscious level, in their future time line. With this creative visualization, clients also reevaluate all events between the current moment and their future goal to ensure that their goal is supported. The unconscious mind will then look for ways to support the goal. Tony Robbins says that 80% of success in anything is psychological and the remaining 20% is mechanics. It is amazing that God created us so that our mind does not distinguish between something we vividly imagine and something we experience. **Our brain does not know the difference between reality and imagination.** Napoleon Hill reportedly said, "Whatever the mind of man can conceive and believe, it can achieve." Perhaps that is one reason why there are many scriptures that address where our thoughts need to be. Thus, we can capitalize on God's design so that we can create the amazing future that we envision and that He desires for us!

God has spoken on what scientists, researchers, mental health practitioners, coaches, and the developers of the NLP and Time Line Therapy® transformation process have shared with us. The following are a few scriptures related to and supporting requisite one: eliminating toxic emotional residue and limiting beliefs; setting values; and setting our minds on the future we wish to create. Please take time to meditate and reflect upon the following scriptures as you continue your personal growth plan of action!

Psalm 16:7	Matthew 15:11	2 Corinthians 10:3-5
Psalm 19:12, 14	Mark 7:20-23	Ephesians 4:31-32
Psalm 51:6	Luke 24:45	Philippians 4:4-7
Psalm 139:23–24	Acts 8:21-23	2 Timothy 1:7
Proverbs 3:5	Romans 1:28	Titus 1:15
Proverbs 18:8	Romans 7:21-25	Hebrews 4:22
Proverbs 20:30 (ESV)	1 Corinthians 2:16	Hebrews 12:15
Isaiah 53:5	2 Corinthians 4:4	
Daniel 2:30	2 Corinthians 5:17	

Reflection:

We need God! We need our hearts and minds to be transformed! We need the 95% unconscious control to be transformed. Which scriptures resonated with you regarding the need to eliminate toxic emotional residue and limiting beliefs/ decisions connected to past events; set values; and create our future?

_____

_____

_____

_____

_____

_____

Taking Radical Action (Includes Enforcing Your Boundaries)

We all are familiar with God's call to repentance (which includes taking radical action). The NIV includes the word "repent" 78 times (www.biblegateway.com). Those scriptures hold a wealth of information, and our brother in Christ Edward J. Anton published an entire book on the subject entitled *Repentance: A Cosmic Shift of Mind and Heart* (2016). Of course, we cannot do justice to such a topic in one section of a chapter, but I will note a few things. I am sure that you can think of many scriptures in which God calls us to have cosmic shifts in our minds and hearts and to follow those shifts up with action. Sometimes, disciples can think that with baptism we are automatically transformed into new creations and that there is little else we need to do. Many think that our challenges, character deficits, and lack of relationship skills just disappear in the waters of baptism—until reality sets in and we face challenges after baptism. Of course, we know that we don't earn our salvation (Ephesians 2:8). Yet, despite this being a controversial topic, the Bible is clear that if we don't obey God's word, we will not keep our salvation (Matthew 7:21; Hebrews 10:26–27; 1 Timothy 4:16; John 14:23; 1 John 2:17; Matthew 7:24–27). God says that we must work out our salvation. The second requisite for change requires that we take massive and relentless action. This is our biblical and psychological recipe for success. The famous businessman and coach, Tony Robbins, graced us with the thought that knowledge is NOT power; execution is the ultimate power.

We have likely heard and read James 1:23–25 countless times:

> *For if anyone is a hearer of the word and not a doer, he is like a man who looks intently at his natural face in a mirror. For he looks at himself and goes away and at once forgets what he was like. But the one who looks into the perfect law, the law of liberty, and perseveres, being no hearer who forgets but a doer who acts, he will be blessed in his doing. (ESV)*

Once again, I looked up the scripture in multiple Bible versions. The Message version was poignant:

> *Don't fool yourself into thinking that you are a listener when you are anything but, letting the Word go in one ear and out the other. Act on what you hear! Those who hear and don't act are like those who*

glance in the mirror, walk away, and two minutes later have no idea who they are, what they look like.

But whoever catches a glimpse of the revealed counsel of God—the free life!—even out of the corner of his eye, and sticks with it, is no distracted scatterbrain but a man or woman of action. That person will find delight and affirmation in the action.

The phrases that stood out to me in this passage are "forgets what he was like," "law of liberty," "the free life," and "perseveres." I always wanted to better understand "forgets what he was like," so I looked up the scripture in the 60 different Bible versions on www.biblegateway.com. Here is some of what I found for James 1:23–25:

"Forgets what he was like" in other Bible versions:
- forgets what sort of person he was (NET Bible)
- he can't see himself anymore or remember what he looks like (TLB)
- he goes on with whatever he was doing without the slightest recollection of what sort of person he saw in the mirror (PHILLIPS)
- You go away and immediately forget how bad you looked (ERV)
- forgets what kind of person he was (CSB)
- forgets what he was like (AMPC)
- immediately forgets what he looked like (AMP)
- forgetteth what manner of man he was (BRG)
- you go out and forget your divine origin (TPT)
- forget who they are and what they look like (VOICE)

"Law of liberty" in other Bible versions:
- law of freedom (PHILLIPS)
- God's perfect law that makes people free (ICB)
- perfect law of liberty (GNV)
- perfect law that sets you free (CEV)
- law that is all right (WE)

"Perseveres" in other Bible versions:
- fixes his attention there (NET Bible)
- remains committed to it (ISV)

- He continues to study it. He listens to God's teaching and does not forget what he heard. (ICB)
- put it into practice (GNT)
- they actually do what God's laws say (GW)
- continueth therein (GNV)
- pay attention to it. If you do what it says (ERV)
- abides in [it] (DARBY)
- if you listen and obey (CEV)
- and continues, becoming not a forgetful hearer but a doer of the work it requires (CJB)
- continue to do it; they put it into practice in their lives (CEB)
- is faithful to it and perseveres in looking into it (AMPC)
- faithfully abides by it (AMP)
- being not a hearer that forgetteth but a doer that worketh (ASV)
- faithfully abides by it, not having become a [careless] listener who forgets but an active doer [who obeys] (AMP)
- continue to study it [persevere in it] (EXB)
- keep on paying attention to it and...put it into practice (GNT)
- makes a habit of so doing (PHILLIPS)
- keeps looking steadily (TLB)
- abides by it (NASB 1995)
- does not forget it will do what it says and be happy as he does it (NLV)
- goes on with it (NTE)
- there remaining (OJB)
- are fascinated by and respond to the truth they hear and are strengthened by it (TPT)
- pursue that path and actually do what God has commanded (VOICE)
- remembers it (WE)
- dwelleth in it (WYC)

Reflection:

Which phrases from the different Bible versions of James 1:23–25 helped you to better understand what God is communicating about taking massive and relentless action?

_____

_____

_____

_____

_____

What are the results of taking massive and relentless action toward God's will (revealed in the Bible [v. 25])?

_____

_____

_____

In what areas of your emotional and spiritual life do you need to take massive and relentless action toward transformation, emotional intelligence, and freedom?

_____

_____

_____

The following are a few additional scriptures related to and supporting requisite two: taking radical action. Please take time to meditate and reflect upon these scriptures as you continue your personal growth plan of action!

Proverbs 1:23	Luke 3:8	2 Corinthians 7:9
Isaiah 30:15	Luke 13:3, 5	2 Timothy 1:7
Isaiah 61:1	Luke 15:7, 10	2 Timothy 1:16, 17
Jeremiah 15:19–21	Acts 3:19	Hebrews 6:1
Jeremiah 18:8	Acts 11:18	James 1:22
Jeremiah 20:12	Acts 17:30	1 Peter 1:13
Jeremiah 31:19	Acts 20:21, 28	1 Peter 2:2
Matthew 3:2, 8	Acts 26:20	2 Peter 3:9
Matthew 6:33–34	Romans 2:4	Revelation 2:16
Matthew 12:43–45	1 Corinthians 13:4–7	Revelation 3:19

Reflection:

Which scriptures helped you to better understand what God is communicating about taking massive and relentless action?

_____

_____

_____

_____

_____

_____

In reference to enforcing our boundaries, I heard a wonderful explanation of how we each have "boundaries" when someone visits our home. Typically, if we are having company, we allow guests to spend time in the living, family, and dining rooms, the kitchen and the bathroom. Unless they are family or close friends, they usually are not allowed in our bedrooms or private bathrooms. This is an example of how we need healthy boundaries or limits in our homes and in every area of our lives. We need healthy boundaries with family, friends, coworkers, schoolmates, business associates, and anyone with whom we have a relationship. Our boundaries include how we allow people to treat us, how we allow people to behave around us, and our expectations in relationships.

Henry Cloud and John Townsend have published seven invaluable books in their boundaries series and even have a boundaries quiz on their website (www.boundariesbooks.com). I cannot write another "Life without" chapter about boundaries, but I have personally seen people without boundaries carry frustration, displaced and/or seething anger that is ready to explode, intense fear (of rejection or abandonment), debilitating anxiety, hurt, depression, deep shame, and guilt. Typically, "people pleasers" do not have healthy boundaries. One without healthy boundaries will likely be controlled and abused by those around them. Decision-making can be difficult. Those without healthy boundaries frequently consider themselves victims and feel annoyed and disrespected. Since they routinely do not speak up for themselves, passive aggressiveness and annoyance can be evident. For us to be transformed, our boundaries need to be brought under the lordship of Jesus, just like everything else.

The following are a few additional scriptures related to and supporting requisite two: enforcing boundaries. Please take time to meditate and reflect upon these scriptures as you continue your personal growth plan of action!

Psalm 16:6	Matthew 5:37	Ephesians 5:1-4
Proverbs 3:11–12	Matthew 10:16	2 Thessalonians 5:1
Proverbs 4:23	1 Corinthians 15:33	Titus 2:14–15
Proverbs 15:25	2 Corinthians 8:13–14	
Jeremiah 5:22–23, 25	Galatians 6:5	

Reflection:
Which scriptures helped you to better understand what God is communicating about enforcing boundaries?

_____

_____

_____

_____

_____

_____

_____

_____

_____

Focusing on What You Want (Your Evaluations Become Suggestions to the Unconscious Mind)

Mahatma Gandhi is noted to have said, "I will not let anyone walk through my mind with their dirty feet." I think that many times, as adults, we provide the dirty feet to pollute our own minds more than those around us do. Though the limiting beliefs (sample list at the beginning of Chapter 9) were typically installed when we were children, they are frequently carried into adulthood. This mental and emotional baggage negatively impacts our current lives. In Philippians 4:8–9, God instructs us,

> *Finally, brothers and sisters, whatever is true, whatever is noble, whatever is right, whatever is pure, whatever is lovely, whatever is*

admirable—if anything is excellent or praiseworthy—think about such things. Whatever you have learned or received or heard from me, or seen in me—put it into practice. And the God of peace will be with you.

Not only do scientists, psychologists, and many preachers note the impact of "positive thinking," but God is the author of it all. As discussed in Chapter 4, our unconscious mind stores all memories, controls and maintains all perceptions, and needs repetition until a habit is installed. If we have stored and continue to repeat toxic emotional residue and limiting beliefs, we must begin by eliminating them. Then we need to **change our focus and all the messages we allow our unconscious mind to store.**

So, what does this look like? How can we turn limiting beliefs/decisions and negative emotional residue into a focus on what we want instead? We begin by completing the first requisite for change by using Time Line Therapy® to eliminate the toxic emotional baggage and limiting beliefs/decisions connected to past events. Then we must take radical and relentless action (the second requisite). Then, with our internal representations swept clean and with the assumption that we trust God's wisdom and love, we must occupy our minds with godly thoughts of what we and God want (Matthew 12:43–45). We must practice systematic emotional relearning. Albert Bandura, in discussing self-efficacy, notes that our beliefs about our abilities have a profound effect on our abilities (Goleman, 1995). Practically, this means that instead of rehearsing, "I am an addict" or "I struggle with impurity," we rehearse, "I am a conqueror; I am victorious; I have self-control; I have healthy connections; I have healthy coping mechanisms," etc. Instead of rehearsing, "I am insecure" or "I am not enough," we reject those evaluations and messages to our unconscious mind and replace them with, "I am God's beloved child; I am secure; I am courageous; I am powerful; I am full of God's Spirit; I am totally accepted," etc.

Instead of allowing our mind to accept the feeling of being stuck with a bad situation, we delete that cognition and replace it with "I am empowered; I set healthy boundaries; I make my own decisions; I work toward God's plan for my life and loved ones; God has given me a spirit of power," etc. Instead of allowing fear and anxiety to control us to the point that we are afraid of being alone, afraid of taking risks, afraid of being rejected, afraid of failure, afraid of vulnerability, afraid of or anxious about what is in the future (e.g., today or next year), and afraid of pain, we scratch those thoughts and feelings. We replace them with "I am courageous; I am in green pastures beside quiet waters (Psalm 23); I choose peace and serenity; I am confident; I am faithful; I am protected; I trust God my provider; I choose joy and love," etc.

Instead of thinking and having internal representations that support feeling like damaged goods, we consider what is true, noble, excellent, praiseworthy, lovely, and admirable (Philippians 4:8–9) about how God created us. Instead of repeating the diagnosis of "I am depressed," after we have eliminated all the sadness and grief connected to past events, we can choose to focus on what we want instead. We can consider and meditate on God's goodness, love, and grace. We can focus on God's amazing plan for our lives now and for eternity. We can choose an emotional state of joy, hope, optimism, happiness, and health. Also, as opposed to using anger as a protective mechanism, we figure out our primary emotions (search for the Anger Iceberg image using an internet search engine of your choice) and assure ourselves that with God, we can effectively handle any emotion, relationship, or situation with godliness and appropriate vulnerability.

Rather than accepting communication problems, psychosomatic illnesses, a lack of relationships, low motivation levels, dysfunctional thinking and behaviors, codependent enabling, unrealistic expectations, or any undesirable schema, we focus on what we want, reject negative evaluations, and feed our unconscious mind the positive nourishment it needs for our future success. With our neuroplasticity, Bruce Lipton notes that we can decide to create new inner and outer worlds. Those are just a few examples of how we can practically master our mind. We can change the way we feel by how we think (Figure 4.2). For every issue listed in the table at the beginning of Chapter 9 ("Time Line Therapy® – Transforming Our Neurology"), we can decide to focus on the future we want to create in the context of our relationship with God. Joe Dispenza notes that going from the old self to the new self and stepping into the uncertainty is the biological, neurological, chemical, and hormonal genetic death of the old self. In Romans 8:12–14, God calls us to put to death the misdeeds of the body and live as His children. The best way for us to predict our future is to use God's power to create it (Romans 8:11). We unconsciously eliminate our limiting beliefs in the first requisite (using Time Line Therapy®) and then consciously choose to cognitively reframe temptations of any unwarranted and inappropriate emotions and beliefs on a daily basis. When we add the power of prayer and the armor of God, we can be as bold as lions (Proverbs 28:1)! With God's Holy Spirit and Time Line Therapy®, there truly are miracles. Our lives continue to transform with the mental and emotional work on our part.

The following are a few additional scriptures related to and supporting requisite three: focusing on what you want—your evaluations become suggestions to the unconscious mind. Please take time to meditate and reflect upon these scriptures as you continue your personal growth plan of action!

Joshua 1:8	Mark 11:23	Philippians 3:7–13
Psalm 1:2	Luke 24:38	Colossians 3:2
Proverbs 4:23 (ESV)	Romans 7:25-26	1 Peter 4:7
Isaiah 26:3	Romans 8:5–7	
Matthew 21:22	Philippians 3:7–13	

Reflection:
Which scriptures helped you to better understand what God is communicating about focusing on what we want and our evaluations, which are suggestions to our unconscious mind?

_____

_____

_____

_____

_____

_____

_____

_____

_____

Romans 12:2
In summary, we are all familiar with Romans 12. It is considered by many to be one of the most important and foundational chapters in the New Testament. I recall in my early walk as a disciple having a class on the book of Romans during which we memorized Romans 12—yes, the entire chapter! Many are familiar with the NIV translation of Romans 12:2 – "Do not conform to the pattern of this world, but be transformed by the renewing of your mind. Then you will be able to test and approve what God's will

is—his good, pleasing and perfect will." Below are some of the other Bible versions for this powerful scripture:

Do not be conformed:
- Be not fashioned (ASV)
- Fashioned after and adapted to its external, superficial customs (AMPC)
- Don't be like the people of this world (CEV)
- Don't change yourselves to be like the people of this world (ERV)
- Do not be shaped by [...pressed into a mold by] (EXB)
- Fashion not yourselves like unto this world (GNV)
- Don't become like the people of this world (GW)

Be transformed:
- be transformed and progressively changed as you mature spiritually (AMP)
- Changed (AMPC)
- Be reformed (DRA)
- Let God change you inside (ERV)
- Be changed within (EXB)

Renewing of your mind:
- Focusing on godly values and ethical attitudes (AMP)
- By its new ideals and its new attitude (AMPC
- Let God change the way you think (CEV)
- Be reformed in the newness of your mind (DRA)
- With a new way of thinking (ERV)
- Change the way you think (GW)

Reflection:
How have the different versions of Romans 12:2 helped you to understand what Paul was communicating?

_____

_____

_____

What decisions will help you grow in your spiritual transformation, emotional in-

telligence, and freedom?

_____

_____

_____

What plans will you develop and what actions will you take today toward greater spiritual maturity and emotional intelligence and freedom?

_____

_____

_____

Is There Anything Helpful
Outside God's Word?

For since the creation of the world God's invisible qualities—his eternal power and divine nature—have been clearly seen, being understood from what has been made.
—Romans 1:20

For in him all things were created: things in heaven and on earth, visible and invisible, whether thrones or powers or rulers or authorities; all things have been created through him and for him.
—Colossians 1:16

Through him all things were made; without him nothing was made that has been made.
—John 1:3

"You are worthy, our Lord and God,
to receive glory and honor and power,
for you created all things
and by your will they were created
and have their being."
—Revelation 4:11

Yet for us there is but one God, the Father, from whom all things came and for whom we live; and there is but one Lord, Jesus Christ, through whom all things came and through whom we live.
—1 Corinthians 8:6

For those of us who have decided that the Bible is the standard for our lives, we have resolved that if something we hear, read, see, or think we experience doesn't match up with God's word, we choose God's word! We choose His word over our feelings/emotions. We choose it over authorities. We choose God's word over political or national affiliations. We even choose God's word over the law—for instance when the law considers something legal, but God considers it sin.

I have met more than a few people who want to hear sermons, classes, messages, or even general information ONLY from the Bible. They want to only listen to the Bible. They do not want to hear anything from science. Even more extreme, some people do not want to hear anything from doctors—as in God will heal your infection (or cancer), so no need to go to the doctor. **Many more believe that God will heal or fix emotional and mental health issues and that there is no need to see a psychiatrist or therapist.** Even more people believe that God will magically fix social (relationship management) dysfunctions once someone makes a commitment to Christ and is baptized. We sometimes seem to believe that folks who did not have relationships (let alone healthy relationships) before becoming disciples will all of a sudden know how to navigate relationships in the church and reach out to others to help them become stronger disciples.

In my master's level coursework for licensing as a therapist, we were required to take a course on the integration of Christianity/theology and psychology. I may have given away the philosophy of many universities and the Liberty University counseling department, but this consideration is extremely important. Should there be an integration of psychology and theology? Should there be an integration of Christianity and any science? Should we be open to information "outside" God's word? Should those with asthma seek treatment from a physician? Those with diabetes? Should those who need eyeglasses depend upon the centuries of research that has led to the many options available today? Should someone who needs intervention for heart disease rely on the doctors that have scientifically studied hearts and relied on secular textbooks? Should we expect the mechanic to share scriptures as s/he fixes our car or the barber or hairstylist to shout hallelujah as they give us our favorite style? Does our mental health counselor need to give us five scriptures with each session? Or should our church, lessons, and personal discipling times address not only the spiritual issues that we face, but also the social, emotional, psychological, physical, financial, vocational, etc.? Should we understand, love, and serve the "whole person" or just the spiritual aspects of each person (Christian or non-Christian)?

Long before formally studying psychology at Liberty University, I was very encouraged by our brother in Christ, Glen Geeting. He not only attempted to help brothers grow spiritually, but he invested hours and hours into also helping those he loved and supported to be more excellent in every area of their lives (finances, professional, relationships, household, etc.). His heart was like that of Paul. I also love the example Paul set when he told Timothy (in 1 Timothy 5:23) to "stop drinking only water, and use a little wine because of your stomach and your frequent illnesses." Paul addressed Timothy's health—he recommended a medicinal solution to Timothy's problem. Somehow, Paul knew, not from biblical scrolls, that fermented wine (or unfermented grape juice) would possibly help. Paul shared helpful information that was not specifically stated in Old Testament scriptures. Paul loved Timothy—all of Timothy. He cared not just about Timothy's spirituality and ministry but also about his physical infirmities. With this 1 Timothy 5:23 directive, Paul even went against the common practices of the Essenes and other Jewish ascetic sects who avoided any semblance of the overuse of beverages that would intoxicate.

Should our church lessons address only spiritual issues and only rely on the Bible? Or are all our God-given human components connected and interdependent? If someone does not have food, shelter, and safety, how well will they be able to focus on their spiritual health? As many of you may know, Maslow's hierarchy is a motivational theory on human needs. Typically, the lower needs on the hierarchy must be satisfied before we attempt to address the higher needs. From the bottom of the pyramid or hierarchy to the top, the needs are physiological, safety, love and belonging, esteem, and self-actualization. We need only to think of how well we function, interact, think, and focus when we are hungry, sleep deprived, or do not feel safe. If there are deficiencies in the basic four needs, it will be more difficult to focus on growth needs. As disciples, we also know that humans can be "rich" in the basic needs but be "bankrupt" spiritually. Amen that we can multitask and keep God at the center and as the foundation of our own needs and the needs of our loved ones.

Jesus Addressing Wholistic Needs

I think of Jesus feeding the hungry. He addressed physical needs. There are many scriptures that show God's heart for the physical aspects of our being and for meeting physical needs. Culminating in Genesis 47, in the midst of a famine, God made a way to meet the food (physical) needs of Joseph's family, the Israelites, and the Egyptians. Throughout the Old Testament, God took care of the priests' physical needs through the tithing of the rest of the nation. In Matthew 19, Jesus challenged the rich man to sell his possessions and give to the poor so that he could be perfect and have treasure in heaven. We also know that our bodies are temples. In 1 Corinthians 6:19–20, God says,

> Do you not know that your bodies are temples of the Holy Spirit, who is in you, whom you have received from God? You are not your own; you were bought at a price. Therefore honor God with your bodies.

In James 2:14–17, God provides a plain and simple statement,

> *What good is it, my brothers and sisters, if someone claims to have faith but has no deeds? Can such faith save them? Suppose a brother or a sister is without clothes and daily food. If one of you says to them, "Go in peace; keep warm and well fed," but does nothing about their physical needs, what good is it? In the same way, faith by itself, if it is not accompanied by action, is dead.*

God is clear on our need to focus not only on our spiritual dimension, but also on our own and others' physical aspects. I have heard it said of many "Christians" that we can sometimes be so heavenly focused that we are no earthly good. Amen that Jesus was the example of addressing all the dimensions of what God has so beautifully, fearfully, and wonderfully created (Psalm 139:14).

I also think of Jesus' focus on women: He addressed cultural issues. I think of Jesus' teachings on the poor: He addressed social issues. I think of Jesus going to Mary and Martha when Lazarus died: He addressed emotional issues. I think of Jesus and the deranged man (of the Gerasenes): He addressed possible mental health issues. Jesus even made wine for a wedding. I love how he inserted himself into the culture, cared about people beyond just their spirituality, and shared his life. Paul said that because he loved the Thessalonians so much and cared so deeply for them, he shared not only the gospel but his life as well (1 Thessalonians 2:8). Our Bible heroes addressed all the dimensions of our human nature, not just the spiritual. Of course, if we fell on hard times financially or physically, we would likely not feel loved if someone said, "Go in peace, keep warm and well fed" (James 2:16) and did absolutely nothing about our challenges. We must address all the dimensions of our own being and of those we love if we are loving as God and Jesus loved!

Models of Integration and Interdependence

Integrative approaches to psychology and Christianity: An introduction to worldview issues, philosophical foundations, and models of integration (2010) by David N. Entwistle was a tremendously informative read. I recommend this book if you'd like a deeper look into the ways secular and biblical views can or can't be integrated, depending on people's worldviews. Entwistle notes that the unique perspectives of Christian theology and psychology "provide for a more complete and accurate picture" of human nature "than either of them would provide in isolation" (p. 1). Since God is the Creator of all, including all truth, The Book of his Word, and the Book of his Works (Entwistle), *the artificial dichotomy of things secular and sacred can be avoided.* Though there are varied beliefs within Christianity (including in our fellowship) and among psychological theories, Entwistle notes that biological, psychological, social, cognitive, and spiritual aspects determine human behavior. Entwistle repeatedly drives home the point that the use of both psychological and Christian perspectives provides a "more complete view of humanity" (Entwistle, p. 119). If we desire to be and behave like Jesus in as many ways as possible, we must address not only the spiritual aspects of our lives and of those we love, but also the biological, psychological, social, and cognitive.

Entwistle (2010) provides five models that can help us to reflect upon and understand how we personally view the world. The language of modeling can be somewhat technical, but don't get too bogged down in the terminology. I'll do my best to paint a broad picture, and if you're interested you can dig deeper by reading the book. As an overview, his Enemies model is a non-integrative paradigm. His Spies and Colonialists models are considered manipulative integration paradigms. The Neutral Parties and Allies models are classified as nonmanipulative integration models.

More specifically, Entwistle's Enemies Model is a nonintegrative, antagonistic paradigm where Secular Combatants and Christian Combatants reject, restrict, or exclude "either religious beliefs or the insights of human reason" (Entwistle, 2010, p. 154). Christian Combatants protect religious authority and make pronouncements against what is considered to be corrupt human reasoning. This is what I describe at the beginning of this chapter: Christians who do not believe that there is anything good outside the Bible. Christian Combatants do not accept the Works of God beyond the Book of God. It may be obvious that secular combatants do not accept religious faiths but believe in the "autonomous exercise of human reason" (Entwistle, p. 154). Secular Combatants see religion as the enemy of psychology. These territorial disputes typically have the same casualties as do territorial disputes between countries or socially constructed groups of people. Many times, hostility wins out and the combatants forget what their issue was in the first place, who started the fight, and that the enemy is a human being with some possibly helpful ideas for us all. The goal of combatants typically is to eradicate their enemy along with anything that is related to or drawn from the enemy. "People who subscribe to the Enemies model assume that psychology and religion (or Christianity) are fundamentally incompatible with each other" (Entwistle, p. 156).

Reflection:
In what ways have your values, beliefs, paradigms, schemas, level of tolerance, and biases fit in with the Christian Combatants school of thought?

_____

_____

_____

_____

_____

_____

With Entwistle's **Spies model,** integration is manipulated with selective rejection and plundering—people take what they want and throw out what they don't want. Foreign and Domestic Spies are said to focus on aiding human well-being without a commitment to religion or religious doctrine. With the Foreign and Domestic models, either theology reconstructs psychological processes or vice versa (Entwistle, 2010, p. 154). The manipulated integration **Colonialists model** describes Christians who have allegiance to a religious system and Christian doctrine and behavior. Colonialists appropriate psychological methods or findings that illustrate or further support their Christian worldview. They filter isolated psychological findings with little engagement in psychological discipline or methods.

Reflection:

In what ways have your values, beliefs, paradigms, schemas, level of tolerance, and biases fit in with the Spies or Colonialists schools of thought?

_____

_____

_____

_____

_____

_____

Neutral Parties recognize "the legitimacy of psychology and theology as independent domains. The emphasis is on distinctiveness rather than unity" (Entwistle, 2010, p. 154). This is considered a non-manipulative integration paradigm.

The last model of disciplinary relationship is one that respects The Book of God and The Work of God. With Entwistle's (2010) **Allies as Subjects of One Sovereign model**, "psychological and theological methods are utilized to gain a more holistic and unified understanding of truth" (p. 154). This model is also a nonmanipulative integration paradigm. Adherents recognize "that human purpose is ultimately expressed when we see ourselves in proper relationship to God" (p. 154). Allies are said to discern "the underlying unity of truth" (p. 154) and use it for godly ends. I most appreciated Entwistle's (2010) discussion on how, since we are flawed, finite, and limited, we should in humility consider the fact that our hermeneutics, presuppositions, thinking, theories, and psychological philosophies could be wrong. Thus, all the more need to critically consider all the resources God has provided, not just those in our fellowship or those of the Christian worldview.

Reflection:

Which model do you feel can be most helpful in addressing all the dimensions of our whole being?

_____

_____

_____

Extrabiblical References in the Bible

A dear friend who is planning to be a teacher in our fellowship informed me that there are several references to, direct quotations from, paraphrases of, and allusions to extrabiblical writers and literature in our Bible. If our biblical heroes and writers incorporated helpful information from outside the Jewish and Christian religions, is it OK for us to do the same? Is it OK to read self-change books other than the Bible? Is it OK to read books that don't have the Bible as the foundation of the information shared? Is it OK to work with or use the services of people who do not have the Bible as their standard or who don't connect a Bible verse to the things they attempt to communicate? Like me, you may have run into disciples/Christians who do not read any books besides the Bible. You may have also run into disciples/Christians who, when encouraged to read a helpful book that is not based on our Christian worldview, feel contempt for the writer and the information contained in such a book. Can we learn anything from noncanonical texts? From people who are not disciples of Christ?

Though a more exhaustive list exists, I was intrigued to learn that:

1. The poetry Book of Jashar is mentioned in Joshua 10:13, 2 Samuel 1:18, and in the Septuagint in 1 Kings 8:53.

2. The Book of the Wars of the Lord is referenced in Numbers 21:14.

3. The book of the annals of the kings of Israel and Judah is mentioned in 1 Kings 14:19, 29 and 16:20.

4. The Laments for Josiah are mentioned in 2 Chronicles 35:25.

5. The chronicles/annals of King Ahasuerus are referenced in Esther 2:23, 6:1, and 10:2 and in Nehemiah 12:23.

It is also believed that the following noncanonical books are referenced in the Old Testament: _Manner of the Kingdom, Book of Songs,_ Acts of Solomon, Annals of King David, Book of Samuel the Seer, Book of Nahan, Book of Gad, Prophecy of Ahijah, Book of Jehu, Story of the Book of Kings, Acts of

Uziah, Ascension of Isaiah, Acts of the Kings of Israel, and Sayings of the Seers. It is reported that the noncanonical Book of Enoch, the Assumption of Moses, and the Epistle to the Laodiceans are mentioned in the New Testament. Menander (1 Corinthians 15:33), Epimenides (Titus 1:12–13), and Aratus (Acts 17:28) are considered pagan authors that are quoted or mentioned in the New Testament (Slick, 2016).

Jesus in His parables used secular examples and information to make spiritual points. Poets and "prophets" of the day are referenced in Acts 17:28, Numbers 21:27, and Titus 1:12. There are more references than I will list here. As I have worked with clients with limited emotional intelligence or health, I have needed to share resources that would likely be helpful for developing this dimension's muscles. A few highly dogmatic disciples have sometimes had trouble accepting the idea that they can learn from writers outside our faith and outside our fellowship. I am grateful for how the Bible writers and even Jesus used resources of their day to help us achieve our goal of understanding, walking with, and being close to God.

Reflection:

Do you require that all knowledge and wisdom come directly from Scripture? Do you believe that doctors, lawyers, physical trainers, mechanics, educators, authors, mental health professionals, professional development providers, tax preparers, or Fortune 500 CEOs have anything helpful to offer even if they are not disciples of Jesus Christ?

_____

_____

_____

Which professionals have you benefited from that are not disciples of Christ?

_____

_____

_____

Allies as Subjects of One Sovereign Model

Entwistle's (2010) model of disciplinary relationship descriptions alone hint at where and how we as Christians and humans can make the most progress and give the most glory to God. We are called to be peacemakers (Matthew 5:9; James 3:18), not enemies. We are called to even love our enemies (Matthew 5:43–44; Luke 6:27, 35). When we who claim to be Christians operate as enemies, we do not represent Jesus' life, and our corporate outreach efforts are harmed (Luke 19:10). Satan disguises, schemes, divides, deceives, and manipulates. We definitely do not want to be in his camp. Entwistle shares that the allies as subjects of one sovereign model "recognizes the underlying unity of human nature and the legitimacy of both theological and psychological investigations" (p. 147).

In this Allies model, when conflicts or incompatibilities arise, adherents seek to analyze theories more thoroughly as opposed to dismissing or demeaning divergent paradigms. As Christians who have a more complete picture of the human experience and who want our entire lives to glorify God, Entwistle points out that we will need to be careful to "distinguish scriptural authority from theological interpretation" (p. 189). We will be better able to fulfill God's will for our lives if we avoid "theological reductionism," in which biological, psychological, and social aspects of human nature are not integrated.

"Morality or spirituality is not the only determinant of psychological health" (Entwistle, p. 171). Indeed, Christians can benefit from the insights of secular individuals—mechanics, barbers, podiatrists, dieticians, personal trainers, and even psychologists and psychiatrists. I often refer to Speech and Arrested Development's song "Mr. Wendal." If we desire to live God's life to the full (John 10:10), and do everything well (Mark 7:37), we can learn from anyone! A character in a movie I recently saw noted that

> the Bible is the word of God. But the word of God cannot be confined to a book. If so, every tree would be a pen and the ink would be the ocean. His word could not be worn out. (*Black & Privileged*)

There is more information about most topics outside the Bible in comparison to what is inside its 66 books. Though it is the most awesome book in history, the Bible is not a medical dictionary, an auto mechanics handbook, a water treatment manual of practice, an emergency management protocol, a sports coaching manual, a human resource policy handbook, or a detailed guide for how we are to recognize, understand, and manage (RUM) our emotions and maintain healthy relationships. Of course, there are biblical principles that can be generalized to most issues in our personal lives, families, churches, and the world today. In order to have healthy relationships and glorify God with every component of our being (spiritual, emotional, mental, professional, etc.), it is very helpful to look both to the Bible and to resources outside the Bible.

In the case of emotional intelligence (encompassing the skills of self-awareness, self-management, social awareness, and relationship management), God has gifted researchers and mental health professionals with the passion and the competence to help us reach our goal of bringing intelligence to our emotions. I pray that this book will also support your continued efforts to glorify God as we work to increase our emotional competencies. I am still on that journey, attempting to reclaim and rebuild years of suppressing emotions and a foundation that did not consider emotional health, healing, or intelligence.

Reflection:

Can you see beyond solely spiritual wellness dimensions and incorporate biological, psychological, social, and even cognitive aspects of your life and the lives of others?

_____

_____

_____

_____

Which of Entwistle's models of disciplinary relationship have you typically adhered to?

_____

_____

_____

_____

Our emotional health and intelligence (the capacity to be aware of, control, and express one's emotions) impacts our relationship with God, ourselves, and others. We can see Matthew 28's "teaching them to obey" command become more of a reality when we are willing and equipped to address all the aspects of the human nature that God has created.

Reflection:

How have you worked on all the dimensions of your human nature (biological, psychological, social, spiritual)? How have you helped others work on all the dimensions of their human nature?

_____

_____

_____

_____

_____

_____

And whatever you do, whether in word or deed, do it all in the name of the Lord Jesus, giving thanks to God the Father through him. (Colossians 3:17)

Bibliography

Alcorn, R. (2011). Emotions: Part of Being Created in God's Image. Retrieved from: https://www.epm.org/blog/2011/May/2/emotions-part-being-created-gods-image

Allender, D. & Longman III, T. (1994). The Cry of the Soul: How Our Emotions Reveal Our Deepest Questions About God. Kindle Edition.

Amen, D. (2005). The Brain and Behavior with Daniel G. Amen, M.D.: A Comprehensive Course on the Neurobiology of Everyday Life. MindWorks Press. Newport Beach, CA.

APA video: High School Psychology: Better Understand Your World. Retrieved from:

https://www.youtube.com/user/TheAPAVideo

Bloom, J. (2012). Your Emotions Are A Gauge, Not a Guide. Retrieved from: https://www.desiringgod.org/articles/your-emotions-are-a-gauge-not-a-guide

Bodenhamer, B. & Hall, L. (1996). Patterns for Renewing the Mind: Christian Communicating & Counseling Using NLP & Neuro-Semantics. Neuro-Semantic Publications. Clifton, CO.

Boeder, E. (2017). Emotional Safety Is Necessary for Emotional Connection. Retrieved from: https://www.gottman.com/blog/emotional-safety-is-necessary-for-emotional-connection/

Bradberry, T. & Greaves, J. (2009). *Emotional Intelligence 2.0*. TalentSmart. San Diego, CA. Kindle Edition.

Brainworks (2019). What are brainwaves? Retrieved from: https://brainworksneurotherapy.com/what-are-brainwaves

Branson, C. (n.d.). Emotional intelligence and our best known Bible characters. Retrieved from: https://www.creedbranson.com/emotional-intelligence-our-best-known-bible-characters/

Campbell, Clark D. and Bufford, Rodger K. A (2012). Christian Perspective on Human Emotions. Faculty Publications, Grad School of Clinical Psychology. 90.

https://digitalcommons.georgefox.edu/gscp_fac/90

Conner, B., Stein, J., & Longshore, D. (2009). Examining self-control as a multidimensional predictor of crime and drug use in adolescents with criminal histories. *Journal of Behavioral Health Services & Research,* April; 36(2): 137–149. doi:10.1007/s11414-008-9121-7.

www.dictionary.com

Dispenza, J. (2018, June 26). The Mind Body Connection. Retrieved from: https://youtu.be/5reo3dXOicU

Dispenza, J. (2019). Healing by Thought Alone. Retrieved from: https://quantumuniversity.com/qu/healing-by-thought-alone/

Eckman, D. (n.d.). The Holy Spirit and our emotions. Retrieved from: https://bible.org/seriespage/holy-spirit-and-our-emotions

Edmiston, J. (2001). Biblical EQ: A Christian handbook for emotional transformation. Retrieved from: http://www.ntslibrary.com/Biblical_EQ_emotional_transformation.pdf.

Elliott, K. (2018). "Challenging toxic masculinity in schools and society," On the Horizon, Vol. 26 Issue:1, pp. 17–22, https://doi.org/10.1108/OTH-11-2017-0088

Entwistle, D. (2010). *Integrative approaches to psychology and Christianity: An introduction to worldview issues, philosophical foundations, and models of integration.* CASCADE Books. Eugene, Oregon.

Gaultiere, B. (n.d.). Transforming your feelings and emotions. Retrieved from: https://www.soulshepherding.org/transforming-feelings-emotions/

GoodTherapy (2015). Time Line Therapy. Retrieved from: https://www.goodtherapy.org/learn-about-therapy/types/timeline-therapy

Goleman, D. (1995). *Emotional Intelligence:* Why It Can Matter More Than IQ. Random House Publishing Group. Kindle Edition.

Got Questions Ministries (n.d.). What is Soul Care. Retrieved from: https://www.gotquestions.org/soul-care.html

Greaves, J., Bradberry, T. & DeLazaro, S. (2011). *Developing Emotional Intelligence@.* San Diego, CA: TalentSmart@.

Greaves, J., Bradberry, T. & DeLazaro, S. (2016). *Mastering Emotional Intelligence@* Level 1. San Diego, CA: TalentSmart@.

Hart, Donna (2016). Emotions: Powerful and Revealing. Retrieved from: https://biblicalcounselingcenter.org/emotions-powerful-revealing/

Human Diseases (n.d.). Emotions. Retrieved from: http://www. humanillnesses.com/Behavioral-Health-Br-Fe/Emotions.html

Itsu Sync (n.d.). Different types of brain waves: Delta, theta, alpha, beta, gamma. Retrieved from: https://itsusync.com/different-types-of-brain-waves-delta-theta-alpha-beta-gamma

James, A. (2013). Time Line Therapy® Made Easy: An Easy Method to Let Go of Negative Emotions and Limiting Decisions from Your Life, Second Edition. Sidonia Press: US.

James, T. (n.d.). NLP Communication Model. Retrieved from: https://www. nlpcoaching.com/nlp-a-model-of-communication-and-personality/

Jones (2014). *Spiritual Maturity: God's Will for Emotional Health and Healing.* Joy Publishing: Boca Raton, FL.

Kuldas, S., Ismail, H. Hashim, S. & Bakar, A. (2013). Unconscious learning processes: mental integration of verbal and pictorial instructional materials. *SpringerPlus 2,* 105 (2013) doi:10.1186/2193-1801-2-105

Kunst, J. (2016). Alpha series: Biblical self-awareness. Retrieved from: https://www.amethystrecovery.org/alpha-series-biblical-self-awareness/

Lehner, Rachel (2016). 20 Verses About God's Plan for Your Welfare, Future, and Hope. Retrieved from: https://unlockingthebible.org/2016/06/20-verses-about-gods-plan-for-your-welfare-future-and-hope/

Lexico (2019). Retrieved from: https://www.lexico.com/en/definition/metacognition

Life application Bible: New international version (1991). Wheaton, IL: Tyndale.

Ligonier Ministries (n.d.). Reformation Study Bible. Retrieved from: https://www.biblegateway.com/passage/?search=rom+7&version=NIV

Lipton, Bruce H. (2016). The Biology of Belief 10th Anniversary Edition. Hay House. Kindle Edition.

Love, Joann (2016). 5 Signs you lack self-awareness. Retrieved from: https://leaderonomics.com/personal/5-signs-you-lack-self-awareness

Mahaney, C. & Mahaney Whitacre, N. (2017). Why Your Emotions Are a Good Thing. Retrieved from: https://www.crossway.org/articles/why-your-emotions-are-a-good-thing/

Mayshar, J. (2018). Why Did God Create Emotions? Retrieved from: https://www.quora.com/Why-did-God-create-emotions

Myles, A. (2015). The Life-changing 90 second street. Retrieved from: https://www.elephantjournal.com/2015/10/the-life-changing-90-second-secret/

Pillay, S. (2018). Brain science to improve your relationships. Harvard Health Blog. Retrieved from: https://www.health.harvard.edu/blog/brain-science-to-improve-your-relationships-2018100414922

Purves, D. Augustine, GJ., Fitzpatrick D. et al., Editors. Neuroscience, 2nd Edition. Sunderland, MA. Sinauer Associates. Retrieved from: https://www.ncbi.nlm.nih.gov/books/NBK10829/

Scazzero, Peter (2003). The Emotionally Healthy Church: A Strategy for Discipleship that Actually Changes Lives. Zondervan, Grand Rapids, MI.

Schomer, A., Morrissey, R. & Noonan, K. (2017). Heal. United States: Elevate Entertainment. https://www.netflix.com/watch/80220013?trackId=13752289&tctx=0%2C0%2C4c1e093e-c52c-4aa5-b7b0-b6b6b35260f8-745555098%2C%2C

Slick, M. (2016). Did Paul quote pagan philosophers? Retrieved from: https://carm.org/did-paul-quote-pagan-philosophers

Tad James Co., LLC (2018). Time Line Therapy® Practitioner Training Manual.

Tad James Co., LLC (2018). Master Time Line Therapy® Practitioner Training Manual.

TalentSmart® & IMPACT EQ Learning (2008). Developing Emotional Intelligence.

Van Der Kolk, Bessel (2014). *The Body Keeps the Score: Brain, Mind and Body in the Healing of Trauma.* Kindle ed., Penguin Books.

www.vocabulary.com

Wake Forest University (n.d.). The difference between feelings and emotions. Retrieved from: https://counseling.online.wfu.edu/blog/difference-feelings-emotions/

Wikipedia (2019). Unconscious mind. Retrieved from: https://en.wikipedia.org/wiki/Unconscious_mind

Wikipedia (2019). Neural oscillation. Retrieved from: https://en.wikipedia.org/wiki/Neural_oscillation

Wilding, Melody (2019). 11 Questions Self-Aware Leaders Should Ask Themselves Daily. Retrieved from: https://medium.com/swlh/11-questions-self-aware-leaders-should-ask-themselves-daily-f96e3c664eee

Williams, S. (2011). Toward a theology of emotion. Retrieved from: https://www.biblicalcounselingcoalition.org/2011/07/27/toward-a-theology-of-emotion/

Without emotional intelligence and personal growth, our lives will be like the seed that fell among thorns (Luke 8:14). We will not be able to most effectively or spiritually handle life's worries, riches, and pleasures, and we will not mature. This book addresses issues that we must consider in order to live as emotionally, spiritually, and relationally mature adults. Not a "quick read" book, it contains scriptures to contemplate, personal sharing, paradigm-changing insights, and reflection questions.

$14.99 at www.ipibooks.com

All these and more available at www.ipibooks.com
Books for Christian Growth from Illumination Publishers

Apologetics

Compelling Evidence for God and the Bible—Truth in an Age of Doubt, by Dr. Douglas Jacoby.
Field Manual for Christian Apologetics, by Dr. John M. Oakes.
Is There A God—Questions and Answers about Science and the Bible, by Dr. John M. Oakes.
Mormonism—What Do the Evidence and Testimony Reveal?, by Dr. John M. Oakes.
Reasons For Belief–A Handbook of Christian Evidence, by Dr. John M. Oakes.
That You May Believe—Reflections on Science and Jesus, by John Oakes/David Eastman.
The Resurrection: A Historical Analysis, by C. Foster Stanback.
When God Is Silent—The Problem of Human Suffering, by Douglas Jacoby.

Bible Basics

A Disciple's Handbook—Third Edition, Tom A. Jones, Editor.
A Quick Overview of the Bible, by Douglas Jacoby.
Be Still, My Soul—A Practical Guide to a Deeper Relationship with God, by Sam Laing.
From Shadow to Reality—Relationship of the Old & New Testament, by Dr. John M. Oakes.
Getting the Most from the Bible, Second Edition, by G. Steve Kinnard.
Letters to New Disciples—Practical Advice for New Followers of Jesus, by Tom A. Jones.
The Baptized Life—The Lifelong Meaning of Immersion into Christ, by Tom A. Jones.
The Lion Never Sleeps—Preparing Those You Love for Satans Attacks, by Mike Taliaferro.
The New Christian's Field Guide, Joseph Dindinger, Editor.
Thirty Days at the Foot of the Cross, Tom and Sheila Jones, Editors.

Christian Living

According to Your Faith—The Awesome Power of Belief in God, by Richard Alawaye.
But What About Your Anger—A Biblical Guide to Managing Your Anger, by Lee Boger.
Called to Be Holy, by Linda Brumley
Caring Beyond the Margins—Understanding Homosexuality, by Guy Hammond.
God, Are We Good? Can I Know for Sure?, by Gordon Ferguson
Golden Rule Membership—What God Expects of Every Disciple, by Dr. John M. Oakes.
How to Defeat Temptation in Under 60 Seconds, by Guy Hammond.
Jesus and the Poor—Embracing the Ministry of Jesus, by Dr. G. Steve Kinnard.
How to Be a Missionary in Your Hometown, by Joel Nagel.
Like a Tree Planted by Streams of Water—Personal Spiritual Growth, by Dr. G. Steve Kinnard.
Love One Another—Importance & Power of Christian Relationships, by Gordon Ferguson.
One Another—Transformational Relationships, by Tom A. Jones and Steve Brown.
Prepared to Answer—Restoring Truth in An Age of Relativism, by Gordon Ferguson.
Repentance—A Cosmic Shift of Mind & Heart, by Edward J. Anton.
Strong in the Grace—Reclaiming the Heart of the Gospel, by Tom A. Jones.
The Guilty Soul's Guide to Grace—Freedom in Christ, by Sam Laing.
The Power of Discipling, by Gordon Ferguson.
The Prideful Soul's Guide to Humility, by Tom A. Jones and Michael Fontenot.
The Way of the Heart—Spiritual Living in a Legalistic World, by Dr. G. Steve Kinnard.
The Way of the Heart of Jesus—Prayer, Fasting, Bible Study, by Dr. G. Steve Kinnard.
Till the Nets Are Full—An Evangelism Handbook for the 21st Century, by Douglas Jacoby.
Walking the Way of the Heart—Lessons for Spiritual Living, by Dr. G. Steve Kinnard.
When God is Silent—The Problem of Human Suffering, by Dr.Douglas Jacoby.
Values and Habits of Spiritual Growth, by Bryan Gray.

Deeper Study

A Women's Ministry Handbook, by Jennifer Lambert and Kay McKean.
After The Storm—Hope & Healing From Ezra—Nehemiah, by Rolan Dia Monje.
Aliens and Strangers—The Life and Letters of Peter, by Brett Kreider.
Crossing the Line: Culture, Race, and Kingdom, by Michael Burns.
Daniel—Prophet to the Nations, by Dr. John M. Oakes.
Exodus—Making Israel's Journey Your Own, by Rolan Dia Monje.
Exodus—Night of Redemption, by Douglas Jacoby.
Finish Strong—The Message of Haggai, Zechariah, and Malachi, by Rolan Dia Monje.
Free Your Mind—40 Days to Greater Peace, Hope, and Joy, by Sam Laing.
In Remembrance of Me—Understanding the Lord's Supper, by Andrew C. Fleming.
In the Middle of It!—Tools to Help Preteen and Young Teens, by Jeff Rorabaugh.
Into the Psalms—Verses for the Heart, Music for the Soul, by Rolan Dia Monje.
King Jesus—A Survey of the Life of Jesus the Messiah, by Dr. G. Steve Kinnard.
Jesus Unequaled—An Exposition of Colossians, by Dr. G. Steve Kinnard.
Mornings in Matthew, by Tammy Fleming.
Passport to the Land of Enough—Revised Edition, by Joel Nagel.
Prophets I—The Voices of Yahweh, by Dr. G. Steve Kinnard.
Prophets II—The Prophets of the Assyrian Period, by Dr. G. Steve Kinnard.
Prophets III—The Prophets of the Babylonian and Persion Periods, by Dr. G. Steve Kinnard.
Remember the Lord—Reflections on Deuteronomy, by Rolan Dia Monje.
Return to Sender—When There's Nowhere Left to God but Home, by Guy Hammond.
Romans—The Heart Set Free, by Gordon Ferguson.
Revelation Revealed—Keys to Unlocking the Mysteries of Revelation, by Gordon Ferguson.
Spiritual Leadership for Women, Jeanie Shaw, Editor.
The Call of the Wise—An Introduction and Index of Proverbs, by Dr. G. Steve Kinnard.
The Cross of the Savior—From the Perspective of Jesus, by Mark Templer.
The Final Act—A Biblical Look at End-Time Prophecy, by Dr. G. Steve Kinnard.
The King Jesus New Testament, by Dr. G. Steve Kinnard.
The Gospel of Matthew—The Crowning of the King, by Dr. G. Steve Kinnard.
The Letters of James, Peter, John, Jude—Life to the Full, by Douglas Jacoby.
The Lion Has Roared—An Exposition of Amos, by Douglas Jacoby.
The Mission—Go and Make Disciples of All Nations, by William and Kristen Lambert.
The Seven People Who Help You to Heaven, by Sam Laing.
The Spirit—Presense & Power, Sense & Nonsense, by Dr. Douglas Jacoby.
Thrive—Using Psalms to Help You Flourish, by Dr. Douglas Jacoby.
What Happens After We Die?, by Dr. Douglas Jacoby.
World Changers—The History of the Church in the Book of Acts, by Gordon Ferguson.

Marriage and Family

A Lifetime of Love—Building and Growing Your Marriage, by Al and Gloria Baird
Building Emotional Intimacy in Your Marriage, by Jeff and Florence Schachinger.
Hot and Holy—God's Plan for Exciting Sexual Intimacy in Marriage, by Sam Laing.
Faith and Finances, by Patrick Blair.
Friends & Lovers—Marriage as God Designed It, by Sam and Geri Laing.
Mighty Man of God—A Return to the Glory of Manhood, by Sam Laing.
Pure the Journey—A Radical Journey to a Pure Heart, by David and Robin Weidner.
Raising Awesome Kids—Being the Great Influence in Your Kids' Lives by Sam and Geri Laing.
Principle-Centered Parenting, by Douglas and Vicki Jacoby.
The Essential 8 Principles of a Growing Christian Marriage, by Sam and Geri Laing.
The Essential 8 Principles of a Strong Family, by Sam and Geri Laing.
The Essential 8 Principles of Christian Parenting, by Sam and Geri Laing.
Warrior—A Call to Every Man Everywhere, by Sam Laing.

www.ipibooks.com

For additional books
from Illumination Publishers go to
www.ipibooks.com